Reading Resource Book

First Steps Second Edition was developed by STEPS Professional Development
(proudly owned by Edith Cowan University) on behalf of the
Department of Education and Training (Western Australia).
It was written by:
Kevlynn Annandale
Ross Bindon
Kerry Handley
Annette Johnston
Lynn Lockett
Philippa Lynch

Second Edition
Addressing Current Literacy Challenges

Authors' Acknowledgements

The *First Steps* team from STEPS Professional Development gratefully acknowledges the contribution made by the following people.

To all the teachers and students who have been involved in trialling the materials and offering feedback as Critical Readers, Test Pilots or Navigator Schools, we give our grateful thanks for your hard work.

The authors of *First Steps* Second Edition gratefully acknowledge and value the work of the authors of the original edition, developed by the Education Department of Western Australia, and the efforts of the many individuals who contributed to that resource.

Contents

Introduction

The *First Steps Reading Resource Book* Second Edition builds on the original *First Steps* text (formerly known as *Reading Resource Book*) by drawing upon contemporary research and developments in the field of literacy learning. This new Resource Book has a strong focus on supporting teachers and schools as they embrace an outcomes-based approach to teaching.

When used in conjunction with the *First Steps Reading Map of Development* Second Edition, the *First Steps Reading Resource Book* Second Edition will provide additional information to enhance teaching and learning at all phases of reading development. It will support teachers to expand their understanding of the four substrands areas—Use of Texts, Contextual Understanding, Conventions and Processes and Strategies. The book focuses on the four substrands and contains practical information on a range of topics including reading procedures, phonological awareness and reading strategies. Each chapter provides a fresh focus for the explicit teaching of reading. All the critical aspects of what, how and why to teach are explained comprehensively. Teachers will find this information extremely relevant for all phases of reading development and will be able to apply the ideas and suggestions as they work with all students in their classroom.

Teachers can move between the *First Steps Reading Map of Development* Second Edition and the *First Steps Reading Resource Book* Second Edition, depending on their particular need and purpose.

CD-ROM icons appear throughout the *First Steps Reading Resource Book* Second Edition. They indicate that a practical format is available on the Reading Strand CD-Rom (included in the *First Steps Reading Map of Development* Second Edition). The CD-ROM is an electronic treasure chest of invaluable activity formats, recording sheets, resource lists and teaching, learning and assessment frameworks.

The *First Steps Linking Assessment, Teaching and Learning* book is also a useful companion to this resource.

CHAPTER 1

Use of Texts

Overview

The Use of Texts substrand focuses on the comprehension and composition of a range of texts. Texts are defined as any form of communication from which meaning is created. This can be spoken, written or visual.

Many categories are used to sort the enormous range of texts that students encounter, for example, fiction and non-fiction, narrative and informational, narrative and expository, literature and mass media. Texts in the *First Steps* resource are classified in three categories — written, spoken or visual. However, each of these categories may be further separated into printed, live and electronic and a text can fall into one or more categories, e.g. **a video is a combination of an electronic, spoken and visual text**.

Students can become both composers and comprehenders of text if they can identify the primary purpose of a text rather than its category. The overview in Figure 1.2 categorises texts according to their purpose.

This chapter provides information about ways to develop students' knowledge and understandings of texts. The four sections are as follows:

- Section 1—Reading Procedures
- Section 2—Developing Fluency
- Section 3—Promoting Reading
- Section 4—Selecting Texts for Students.

Figure 1.1

An Overview of Texts

Modes	MEDIA	Tending Towards Literary Text			PURPOSES	Tending Towards Informational Text				FORMATS
		Entertain	Recount	Socialise	Inquire	Describe	Persuade	Explain	Instruct	
Written	Printed	Narrative Poem Song lyric Fairytale Fable Myth	Biography Autobiography Diary Journal Retelling personal experience	Invitation Apology Message Note Personal correspondence	Survey Questionnaire	Report Label Menu Contents page Index Glossary	Exposition Menu Job application Editorial Headlines	Explanation Affidavit Memo Rules Policy Journal Timetable Complaint	Directions Timetable Recipe Manual Invoice List Experiment Summons	Magazine Letter Book Brochure Pamphlet Newspaper Chart Journal
	Electronic	Joke		Chat room						CD-ROM Text Message Email Fax Card
Spoken	Live	Joke Story Song lyric	Conversation	Greeting Apology Telephone conversation	Interview	Oral report	Debate Discussion	Oral explanation	Oral directions	Performance Speech
	Electronic	Talking book Song lyric		Voicemail message			Talkback radio Song lyric			Audio cassette Radio Television CD-ROM Video
Visual	Live	Play Theatre								Clothing Tattoo Gesture
	Printed	Painting Photograph Cartoon	Picture book Photograph			Travel brochure	Logo Advertisement Catalogue	Timeline Graph Table Flowchart	Road sign	Button Flyer Poster Magazine
	Electronic	Television sitcom Film					Advertisement	Documentary News report		CD-ROM Video cassette Web page

Figure 1.2 An Overview of Texts

4

SECTION 1

Reading Procedures

Using a Range of Reading Procedures

The ultimate aim of any reading program is to produce confident, competent and independent readers. The strategic use of a range of reading procedures ensures this as it provides a strong foundation for a comprehensive reading program. Each reading procedure involves varying degrees of responsibility for both the teacher and student. Using a selective range of reading procedures ensures that explicit instruction and guidance, when needed, is balanced with regular opportunities for the independent application of skills and strategies. Once teachers are familiar with a range of procedures, they can determine which procedure will be the most effective to use according to the students' needs, the familiarity of content or the purpose of the reading session.

What Are Reading Procedures?

Reading procedures provide meaningful contexts for focusing on selected parts of the reading process. They are characterised by a number of widely accepted steps or stages, conducted frequently and are generally applicable to all phases of development. Seven reading procedures have been selected as critical to implementing a comprehensive approach to reading. The seven reading procedures are as follows:

- **Reading to Students**
- **Modelled Reading**
- **Language Experience**
- **Shared Reading**
- **Guided Reading**
- **Book Discussion Groups**
- **Independent Reading.**

The inclusion of each procedure has been influenced by the Gradual Release of Responsibility Model (Pearson and Gallagher, 1983; see *Linking Assessment, Teaching and Learning* book, Chapter 7.) Procedures such as Modelled Reading, Reading to Students and Language Experience allow the teacher to demonstrate how strategies can be used to help the reader make sense of text. Shared and Guided Reading provide opportunities for students to practise these strategies with guidance and support. Book Discussion Groups and Independent Reading sessions allow students time to apply what they have learnt about reading.

Although procedures are often perceived as linear and specific, in practice they vary. Not every teacher will conduct a particular procedure in exactly the same way. It is more important that teachers are aware of the essential elements of each procedure. They can then share common notions of accepted practice. Having an understanding of a range of reading procedures also allows teachers to identify how different procedures are related.

Selecting Reading Procedures

When selecting reading procedures, the following questions can help ensure that students gain the maximum benefit from each session.

- What is the purpose of the session?
- Which reading procedure will allow for the appropriate degree of student participation? e.g. **Do students need explicit teaching or time for purposeful practice**?
- What resources will be required?
- How will students be grouped?
- What will be planned for other students while working with a small group?
- What classroom routines are in place to enable students to work independently?

An overview of the procedures appears on the following page (see Figure 1.3) and all procedures are discussed in detail in this section.

Overview of Reading Procedures

	Reading to Students	Modelled Reading	Language Experience	Shared Reading
Definition	• Reading a text aloud to students	• Demonstrating reading behaviours and verbalising the cognitive processes involved with those behaviours	• To use a shared experience as a basis for jointly creating a text that is then used for further reading	• A teacher-managed blend of modelling, choral reading and focused discussion
Key Features	• Primary purpose is to share enjoyment of reading • Reading is uninterrupted • Sessions span 10 to 15 minutes daily	• Clear 'think aloud' statements • Singular or limited focus • Multiple demonstrations • Brief sessions from 5 to 10 minutes	• Based on a Shared Experience • Text created as a result of the experience • Use students' language when creating the text • Use the created text for further reading activities	• Short sessions from 10 to 20 minutes • Singular or limited focus • Text visible and accessible to all • Differentiated activities • Multiple readings of the text

	Guided Reading	Book Discussion Groups	Independent Reading
Definition	• Teacher scaffolds and supports a group of students as they read a common text	• A small group of students who meet to read and discuss a text they have selected	• Students select texts to read by themselves
Key Features	• Clearly defined purpose • A group of students with identified common need • Most reading done silently • A pattern of asking guiding questions, reading, discussing	• Groups are temporary • Students facilitate discussion • Students select texts • Regular meeting time	• Students select texts • Uninterrupted time span

Figure 1.3 Overview of Reading Procedure

Reading to Students

Definition: Reading a text aloud to students

Description

The focus of Reading to Students is on sharing a text for pleasure and not on the explicit teaching of such things as reading strategies, language structures or vocabulary. When Reading to Students, effective reading behaviours and a positive attitude can be demonstrated.

When Reading to Students it is important to choose a wide variety of texts that are within the students' conceptual capacity and texts that will appeal. This will enable students to make personal connections, expand their world knowledge, challenge their thinking and create an emotional response. Encouraging students to recommend or provide texts they have enjoyed is a good source of texts for Reading to Students.

Key Features

• The primary purpose is to share an enjoyment and love of reading.
• Reading is uninterrupted.
• Sessions are most effective when kept to a ten- to fifteen-minute time span on a daily basis.

Benefits for Students

Reading to Students helps students to:
• develop a positive attitude towards reading
• become aware of a range of text forms
• extend their vocabulary
• extend their imagination and generate new ideas
• develop a sense of how texts work
• comprehend challenging or abstract concepts and issues that might be too difficult for independent reading
• learn about different authors, illustrators and their styles
• make personal connections to texts
• listen actively.

Suggestions for Using Reading to Students in the Classroom

Planning for *Reading to Students*

- Pre-read the text to develop familiarity with it and to ensure the text is appropriate.
- Decide how much of the text will be read in the session, e.g. an extract, a chapter or the whole text.
- Consider the students' familiarity with the content or concepts covered in the text. It is worthwhile to encourage discussions before reading to help build prior knowledge and assist understanding if content or concepts are unfamiliar to students.

Conducting *Reading to Students* Sessions

- Introduce the text and explain why it has been chosen.
- Activate the students' prior knowledge. This could be done in a variety of ways such as discussing and predicting from the cover, illustration and title or predicting the content, language and text form.
- Read the text to students. Demonstrate enjoyment, surprise, suspense and any other reactions incurred when reading the text. Avoid interrupting the flow when reading unless the meaning has been lost.
- Allow time for students to reflect on and respond to the reading.

After *Reading to Students*

- Make texts available so students can explore them during other times.
- Be prepared to re-read texts that the class have enjoyed.

Figure 1.4

Ideas for Assessment

During the Reading to Students procedure, make informal observations about the students' behaviours, e.g. **Do they sit and listen to the text? Are they easily distracted? Do they actively participate in discussions?**

Reflecting on the Effective Use of the Reading to Students Procedure

- Do I read to my students daily?
- Do I read a variety of text forms?
- Do I focus on enjoyment when Reading to Students?
- Do I choose texts within the conceptual capacity of the students? If not, do I prepare students for the concepts they will encounter?
- Do I model positive reading behaviours?

Modelled Reading

Definition: Demonstrating reading behaviours and verbalising the cognitive processes involved with those behaviours.

Description

The focus of Modelled Reading is on the explicit planning and demonstration of selected reading behaviours. This regularly includes the demonstration of comprehension and word identification strategies. Students participate by actively listening and watching rather than by contributing, suggesting and pursuing discussion.

Modelled Reading is most effective when used immediately before students are asked to "have-a-go" at using a new reading behaviour. The shared use and practice of new learning by students may not happen immediately and will require many demonstrations.

When using Modelled Reading it is important to choose a text that is most suited to demonstrate the selected reading behaviour. It is also critical to locate a variety of literary and informational texts, that can be used to demonstrate the same behaviour over a series of Modelled Reading sessions. Enlarged texts allow the students to see the text as the teacher reads and thinks aloud.

Key Features

• Clear 'think aloud' statements are used.
• The focus is singular or limited in a session.
• The same behaviour is modelled many times.
• Sessions are most effective when kept brief (five to ten minutes).

Benefits for Students

Modelled Reading helps students to:
• understand how effective readers read and process text
• gain a deeper understanding of when, how and why particular reading strategies are used by effective readers
• see how a particular text form can be read
• build their understanding of the English language
• understand how reading and writing are related.

Suggestions for Using Modelled Reading in the Classroom

Planning for *Modelled Reading*

- Determine the focus of the session and choose a text that allows multiple demonstrations of a particular reading behaviour.
- Pre-read the text to determine the places where a 'think aloud' statement will be used to demonstrate a specific reading behaviour.
- Consider the language that will be used at each selected place in the text.

Conducting *Modelled Reading* Sessions

- Explain to students the reading behaviour that will be demonstrated and why the text was chosen.
- Introduce the text. Pause at a pre-determined place in the text to think aloud and to demonstrate the behaviour.
- Continue explicit demonstrations of the selected behaviour including thinking aloud. Students may ask questions to clarify their understanding of the text; however, the focal point of the session should be the 'thinking aloud' by the teacher.
- After modelling with the text, review the selected focus.
- If appropriate, involve the students in creating a record of the reading behaviours. As only one or two behaviours are usually modelled at any one time, this chart would be cumulative.

After *Modelled Reading*

- After many Modelled Reading sessions with the same focus, it is important for students to take part in Shared, Guided or Independent Reading sessions. These sessions will provide opportunities to practise and apply the new behaviours.

Figure 1.5

Ideas for Assessment

Within the Modelled Reading session, there is little opportunity to gather information about the students. However, during Shared, Guided and Independent Reading sessions teachers will be able to observe students applying previously modelled behaviours.

***Reflecting on the Effective Use
of the Modelled Reading Procedure***

- Did I keep the session short and sharp? (five to ten minutes)
- Did I focus on the selected behaviour?
- Did I use 'think aloud' effectively as part of my demonstration?
- Did the students stay focused and attend to the demonstration?

Language Experience

Definition: To use a shared experience as a basis for jointly creating a text that is then used for further reading.

Description

The focus of Language Experience is on involving students in a shared experience. As a result of the shared experience, oral language is generated and a written text is created. This jointly created text, scribed by the teacher, becomes the text for further reading sessions.

Language Experience opportunities can be generated in a range of ways.

- Planned activities inside the classroom, e.g. bringing in an animal or object to observe and discuss, inviting a guest to class, cooking
- Planned activities outside the classroom, e.g. taking a trip to an interesting location such as the beach, fire station, or zoo
- Unplanned events, e.g. the builders arriving at the school, a stormy day.

Key Features

- The students' oral language forms the basis for creating the written text.
- The Shared Writing procedure can be used to create the text.
- The whole class participates.
- The created text can be used for further reading activities.

Benefits for Students

Language Experience helps students to:

- talk and read about events in which they have participated
- feel 'ownership' of a text
- develop their vocabulary
- build concept and topic knowledge
- build self-confidence in reading
- understand the relationship between speaking, writing and reading.

Suggestions for Using Language Experience in the Classroom

Planning for *Language Experience*

- Decide on a purposeful experience that will interest students.
- Where possible, involve students in the planning, preparation and organisation of the experience, e.g. preparing questions for a guest speaker, sending invitations, making bookings.

Conducting *Language Experience* Sessions

- Share the experience. (If desired, take photographs to record the event.)
- Encourage students to be as involved as possible in the experience ensuring there is lots of experience-centred talk.
- When the experience is completed, discuss the event as a whole class.
- Conduct a Shared Writing session to record the experience.
- Revise and edit the text with students until it is ready to be published.
- Publish the text, e.g. **create a big book, a bulletin board display, an illustrated chart.**
- Involve the students in purposeful reading and re-reading of the text.

After *Language Experience*

- Use the text as a springboard for other reading activities, e.g. **word searches, word sorting, cloze, sequencing, sentence matching.**
- Use the class-made text in Modelled, Shared or Guided Reading sessions.
- Make a copy of the text available for independent use.
- Make small copies of the text so each student can take it home to share.
- Engage students in further purposeful writing activities related to the experience, e.g. **thank you letters, newspaper reports, assembly reports.**

Figure 1.6

Ideas for Assessment

Language Experience sessions enable the teacher to observe individual students as they work as part of the whole class. Valuable information can be gathered about a student by observing their contribution to the Shared Writing, directing particular questions to them or asking them to read sections of the text independently.

Reflecting on the Effective Use of the Language Experience Procedure

- Did I stimulate enough discussion to generate sufficient oral language?
- Did I ask open-ended questions?
- Did I value the students' oral language in the creation of the written text?
- Did I take the opportunity to extend the students' vocabulary?
- Did I use the text for other reading purposes?

Shared Reading

Definition: A teacher-managed blend of modelling, choral reading and focused discussion.

Description

Shared Reading is a supportive, interactive reading procedure where all students can see the text being shared. Students observe a good model (usually the teacher) reading the text and are invited to read along.

Shared Reading provides a common starting point and context for a variety of subsequent whole class literacy activities. Whole class shared reading sessions also provide a springboard for working with smaller groups to extend or consolidate reading behaviours or knowledge at different levels.

Texts selected for Shared Reading sessions need to enable the teacher to demonstrate the chosen reading behaviours. Enlarged texts allow the students to see the text and contribute to the oral reading. Texts can be re-used several times; however it is important to sustain the students' interest and attention when re-visiting the same text.

Key Features

- Sessions are most effective when they are brief. (ten to twenty minutes)
- All students in the class actively participate.
- The focus is singular or limited in one session.
- The text is visible and accessible to all.
- Differentiated activities follow the shared reading.
- There are multiple readings of the text.

Benefits for Students

Shared Reading helps students to:
- be actively involved in reading in a supported way
- understand how texts are read and hear effective reading
- experience success and satisfaction as they become familiar with texts
- access and enjoy texts that may be beyond their independent reading level
- interact with texts at their own level
- develop knowledge of texts and text conventions
- be exposed to a range of text forms.

Suggestions for Using *Shared Reading* in the Classroom

Planning for *Shared Reading*

- Determine the focus of the session and choose a text that allows multiple demonstrations of the focus.
- Pre-read the text.
- Determine the points in the text where the particular focus can be demonstrated.
- Determine the places in the text where the students can participate in choral reading.
- Plan follow-up activities for the whole class, small groups or individual students.

Conducting *Shared Reading* Sessions

- Explain the focus of the session.
- Activate prior knowledge. This could be done in a variety of ways such as inviting students to make predictions about content, discussing the form of the text, looking at illustrations and identifying possible vocabulary.
- Read the whole text focusing on meaning and enjoyment.
- Re-read the text inviting students to participate either in directed parts or as they feel comfortable, e.g. **read a repetitive pattern, join in the reading, complete a rhyming section**.
- After re-reading, return to the text to emphasise a selected focus, e.g. **"Can you find any rhyming words on this page?"**

After *Shared Reading*

- Involve students in whole class, small group or individual practice activities that relate to the selected focus.
- Provide small copies of the text for guided, independent or home reading.
- Provide an audio version of the text for students to listen to or read along with.

Ideas for Assessment

Shared Reading allows the teacher to observe individual students working as part of a whole class. Valuable information can be gathered about a student by observing their participation, directing particular questions to them, or asking them to read a section of the text independently.

**Reflecting on the Effective Use
of the Shared Reading Procedure**

- Did the students actively participate in the reading?
- Could all students clearly see the text?
- Did I keep the sessions focused and was it about ten- to twenty-minutes long?
- Did I select a text that was appropriate for the chosen teaching focus?
- Did I involve the students in meaningful follow-up activities related to the text?

Figure 1.7

Guided Reading

Definition: Providing scaffold and support to a small group of students, with a similar need, as they read a common text.

Guided Reading is sometimes referred to as Directed Silent Reading (DSR), Directed Reading Thinking Activity (DRTA) (Stauffer 1980) or Predicted Substantiated Silent Discourse Reading (PSSDR) (Sloan and Latham, 1981). Reciprocal Reading (Palincsar 1984) is another form of guided reading.

Description

Guided Reading is a procedure that enables teachers to support small groups of students who use similar reading strategies and who are able to read texts at a similar level.

Guided Reading enables students to practise using strategies that have already been introduced. The teacher guides or directs the readers to sections of the text using the following pattern: set a focus question, predict, read and discuss. Most of the reading is performed silently. Reading aloud is reserved for substantiation.

It is essential that the texts used in Guided Reading sessions be selected to match the readers' instructional level and interests. Guided Reading texts need to provide a challenge without being so difficult that readers become discouraged. Selected texts need to be appropriate so they allow students to practise the chosen reading strategies.

Key Features
• Teacher-selected texts are pitched at students' instructional level.
• Small groups of students work with individual copies of the same text.
• Students are grouped to focus on an identified need.
• Most reading is performed silently.
• The teacher guides the reading.

Benefits for Students
Guided Reading helps students to:
• practise and monitor their use of strategies in a supportive setting
• develop confidence in their use of strategies
• refine their understandings about the text as they read
• explore the questions, feelings and ideas about the text
• compare their interpretations of the text with other students.

Suggestions for Using *Guided Reading* in the Classroom

Planning for *Guided Reading*

- Identify a small group of students who have a similar need. The identified need will become the focus of the session.
- Organise other students to work independently.
- Choose a text at the students' instructional level so the focus can be practised.
- Pre-read the text and identify natural breaks where guiding questions can be asked.
- Formulate guiding questions.

Conducting *Guided Reading* Sessions

- Outline the focus of the lesson explaining why it is important for successful reading.
- Activate the students' prior knowledge and supply additional information that will help them relate to the text.
- Pose an initial guiding question related to the focus of the lesson and allocate a section of the text to be read silently.
- Encourage students to share and discuss their responses, ensuring they substantiate their views by returning to the text. Responses may also include discussing the strategies used to find the required information.
- Pose the next guiding question and allocate the section of text. Continue this process until the text has been completed.
- Reflect on the focus of the session and review the initial reason for the reading.

After *Guided Reading*

- Make the text available for independent or home reading.
- Provide practice activities that relate to the selected focus.

Figure 1.8

Ideas for Assessment

Guided Reading allows the teacher to observe individual students as they work in small groups. Information can be gathered about students' reading strategies, comprehension, metacognitive aspects of reading and personal response to the text.

Reflecting on the Effective Use
of the Guided Reading Procedure

- Did I select a text appropriate to the students' instructional level and selected focus?
- Did I select a small group of students with a similar need?
- Did my guiding questions help students practise the identified focus?
- Did I allow the students to read the text silently?
- Did I allow time for students to reflect on their use of reading strategies?

Book Discussion Groups

Definition: Small groups of students who meet to discuss, respond to and reflect on a common text they have chosen to read.

Book Discussion Groups are also known as Book Clubs, Literature Conversations, Socratic Seminars, or Book Talks. Literature Circles (Daniels 1994) is another form of book discussion groups.

Description

The focus of Book Discussion Groups is on a small group of students selecting a text, reading it independently and meeting on a regular basis to discuss it. With certain modifications, Book Discussion Groups are applicable across all year levels and can work equally well with literary and informational texts.

It may be necessary for the teacher to facilitate discussions with younger students, or with students inexperienced or unfamiliar with the procedure. Once students are confident with the Book Discussion Group procedure, several groups within the class may meet simultaneously.

By providing a range of texts to choose from, teachers are able to guide students to select appropriate texts. It is critical that students in each group have an individual copy of the selected text.

Key Features

- Students select their texts.
- Temporary groups are formed based on text choice.
- A pre-determined length of time is allocated for each text, e.g. **five to six weeks**.
- Groups meet on a regular basis for a pre-determined time span.
- Different groups read different texts.
- Students are responsible for being prepared for each meeting.
- The teacher provides support where needed.

Benefits for Students

Book Discussion Groups help students to:
- self-select their reading materials
- read independently
- think critically
- make personal connections
- respond to texts in meaningful ways
- solve problems
- develop questioning skills

- actively participate in student-led group discussions
- collaborate, set goals and pursue their own questions
- appreciate other viewpoints.

Suggestions for Using Book Discussion Groups in the Classroom

Planning for *Book Discussion Groups*

- The process of participating in a book discussion group will need to be modelled several times with the whole class. This could be done by having the whole class read the same text or using a fishbowl[1] technique. It is important to model elements such as generating questions, allocating amounts of text to be read, using roles to promote group discussion and how to prepare for a book discussion meeting.
- A range of charts can be jointly created and prepared to provide scaffolds for students. Figure 1.9, on the following page, demonstrates possible Book Discussion Roles.
- Determine how long and how often students will meet in their groups, e.g. **an hour once a week, thirty minutes twice a week, daily**.
- Set a completion date. Estimate how long it will take students to read and discuss the entire text.
- Decide when reading and preparation for discussions will happen, e.g. **regular classtime, at home or a combination of the two**.
- Decide how many students will be in each group. Groups of four or five students are recommended as this gives all students an opportunity to be involved.
- Choose six to eight diverse texts from which the students can select. Where possible pre-read part or all of the texts to enhance the interaction between students and teacher.
- Decide how students will nominate the text they wish to read, e.g. **ballot with top three choices**.

Conducting *Book Discussion Groups*

- Display texts and give a brief snapshot of each text using the title, author, illustrator, cover and blurb.
- Allow students to nominate the text they wish to read and form them into small groups. Group members' first task is to allocate roles and decide how many pages are to be read before they meet for their first discussion.

---

[1] A Fishbowl technique involves students seated around the perimeter of the room observing a group rehearsing the process. The teacher directs observations and facilitates discussion about the process being used.

- Have students read the designated pages independently and prepare for the meeting. Provide students with sticky notes to make recordings during their reading.
- Organise a time for book groups to meet to discuss their text. Move around the room offering advice or observing student behaviours. It is important not to become actively involved in the discussions.
- At the conclusion of the meetings, direct students to allocate new roles and decide how many pages they will read before the next discussion group takes place.
- Gather the whole class together to reflect on the issues and successes of their group meeting.

After *Book Discussion* Groups

- Provide time for the students to write in their response journals or reading logs.
- Once the entire text is completed allow students to respond to the text, individually or as a group demonstrating their understanding or appreciation of the text.
- Encourage students to search for and participate in suitable online Book Discussion Groups. A search of 'book discussion groups for children' reveals several sites, many from public libraries and book publishers. Care needs to be taken that any sites students access are bona fide.

Questioner	**Interesting Word Finder**
Selects or generates questions that will lead the group discussion.	Locates interesting words within the text prior to the meeting.
Asks the questions to the group.	Researches information about each word.
	Shares their findings with the group.

Possible
Book Discussion Roles

Summariser	**Manager**
Summarises the section of the text that has been read by the group.	Keeps an eye on the time.
	Ensures that all members of the group contribute.
Summarises the group's thoughts at the end of each question.	Leads the decision-making about the tasks for the next meeting.
	Allocates new roles for the next meeting.

Figure 1.9 Possible Book Discussion Roles

Ideas for Assessment

During a Book Discussion Group session there are opportunities to observe group discussions, noting individual student's reading or social behaviours as well as group interaction. Periodically collecting students' response journals or reading logs will provide information about their understanding of the text. Student self-evaluations or reflection sessions may provide insights into the way groups are working and the goals they are setting.

Reflecting on the Effective Use of the Book Discussion Group Procedure
• Did I act as a facilitator and not the director of the discussion during student meetings?   • Did I introduce the essential processes required for students to fully participate in Book Discussion Groups?   • Did I allow students to select the text from the range provided?   • Did I provide time for students to reflect on their participation in the Book Discussion Group?   • Did I allocate sufficient time for students to complete the text?

Independent Reading

Definition: The independent application of previously learnt reading strategies to a self-selected text.

Independent Reading may be known as: USSR—Uninterrupted Sustained Silent Reading, SSR—Sustained Silent Reading, DEAR—Drop Everything and Read, DIRT—Daily Independent Reading Time.

Description

The focus of Independent Reading is students taking charge of their own reading—they choose their own texts, read silently and take responsibility to work through any challenges presented by the text.

Independent Reading for readers who are unable to accurately read the print is still possible. It could take the form of looking at the pictures and 'telling the story' or sitting with a partner and sharing a text. During such sessions the noise level may rise but as long as this is kept at an acceptable level, students are fostering a love and enjoyment of reading.

When using Independent Reading, the responsibility for choosing the text is in the hands of each student. While students are free to choose the texts they prefer, they can be encouraged to select a wide variety of literary and informational texts.

Key Features

• Students select their own text.
• Everyone is involved in reading.
• The session is uninterrupted.

Benefits for Students

Independent Reading helps students to:
• read texts for enjoyment
• apply reading strategies
• re-read texts with which they have previously worked
• pursue their favourite authors or text forms
• select texts that match their interests.

Suggestions for Using Independent Reading in the Classroom

Planning for *Independent Reading*

- Ensure there is a range of reading material available.
- Establish routines for Independent Reading, e.g. **borrowing system, seating arrangement, noise level**.
- Teach students how to select texts. Jointly construct a class chart and have students refer to it when necessary.
- Ensure the text organisation system is clearly understood.
- Allocate time each day for Independent Reading.

Conducting *Independent Reading* Sessions

- Re-iterate the routines for Independent Reading.
- Have students select their own text.
- Have everyone read for the allocated time.
- Provide time for students to reflect on their reading.

After *Independent Reading*

- Provide opportunities for students to respond to the text, e.g. **write in reading journal, discuss with a partner**.

Figure 1.10

Ideas for Assessment

Independent Reading allows teachers to observe individual students as they read. Information can be collected about students' self-selection of reading material, reading behaviours and attitude.

Reflecting on the Effective Use of the   ***Independent Reading Procedure***
• Did I set aside an uninterrupted period of time each day for Independent Reading?   • Did I encourage all students to read independently?   • Did I allow students to choose their own reading materials?   • Did I read? If not, did I use the time to observe and gather information about the students?   • Did I introduce the essential processes needed for Independent Reading?

SECTION 2

Developing Fluency

What Is Fluency?

Fluency is the ability to read aloud with expression to demonstrate an understanding of the author's message. Fluency includes the elements of intonation, phrasing, syntax and accuracy. A fluent reader pays attention to the graphic, syntactic and semantic elements of the text. Fluency is much more than the accurate recognition of individual words on the page. In order to be truly fluent, a reader comprehends the author's message and then conveys his or her interpretation to others.

Research has indicated that fluent reading and good comprehension go together. (Armbruster *et al.* 2001) Although there is no evidence to suggest that there is a causal relationship between comprehension and fluency, those students who scored higher on measures of fluency also scored higher on measures of comprehension. One theory about the correlation between the two is that when fluent readers read text they are able to concentrate on the meaning, as they do not need to spend time and effort decoding the words on the page. This implies that fluent readers have an extensive sight vocabulary, which they use successfully.

Helping Students to Become Fluent Readers

In order to read fluently, students must first hear and understand what fluent reading sounds like. Teachers can demonstrate this by reading aloud often and from a great variety of texts. Modelling of fluent oral reading is both a demonstration and a discussion of what, how, when and why. According to Worthy and Broaddus (2001)

> "Students who feel in control of their own learning, who know why fluency is important and what can be done to improve it, are more likely to engage in the kinds of repeated practice that leads to fluency."

When modelling oral reading and thinking aloud, teachers can discuss a variety of aspects.

- **Phrasing**—"Did you hear how I grouped these words together when reading? That's because they all go together as a phrase."

- **Punctuation** and its effects—"Did you hear how my voice went up slightly at the end? That's because the author has put a question mark here."
- **Typographical aids** such as bold type or italics—"Did you hear how I said this word loudly. That's because the author has put it in bold type so she wants to emphasise this word."

Fluent oral reading behaviours can be brainstormed after modelling sessions. These can be referred to before and during further oral reading sessions.

A Fluent Oral Reader
• reads and re-reads the text • uses different facial expressions to show mood • looks up from the text to make eye contact with the audience • reads groups of words together • changes voices for different characters • voice rises and falls to show different moods.

Figure 1.11 Fluent Oral Reading Chart

Teachers can also provide opportunities for students to hear other models of fluent oral reading. These could include other adults such as parents and teacher assistants. Other students such as buddies or more able readers in the class can also be models. Other sources are CD-ROMs or book and tape sets that provide students with a variety of efficient reading models.

Providing Opportunities for Repeated Reading

Apart from providing good models of oral reading to help develop fluency, students benefit from reading aloud themselves. Teachers often provide students with some form of supported oral reading that enables them to re-read texts. Oral reading opportunities in the classroom can go beyond the round robin format.

When a reader is unprepared for oral reading, he or she may feel anxious or embarrassed. Listening to unprepared oral reading can also cause the listener to become frustrated and inattentive. Effective oral reading needs to be purposeful and accompanied by constructive feedback. A variety of opportunities for repeated readings, beyond the round robin reading model, will help students develop fluency in a non-threatening and supportive environment.

The following provide opportunities for repeated readings.

1 **Echo Reading**
2 **Shadow Reading**
3 **Assisted Reading**
4 **Shared Reading**
5 **Choral Reading**
6 **Tape-assisted Reading**
7 **Readers' Theatre**
8 **Radio Reading**
9 **Poetry Club**
10 **Buddy Reading**

1 Echo Reading

The teacher works with small groups reading a text, sentence by sentence. After the teacher reads each sentence, the students are encouraged to read the same sentence. This activity can be performed frequently but it is important to keep the sessions relatively short.

- Read the first sentence of a text or short paragraph, demonstrating fluency and expression. Have students follow along. The sentence may need to be re-read depending on the experience of the students or the text.
- With the students, re-read the sentence using the same fluency and expression.
- Have students re-read the sentence fluently by themselves. It is important to give feedback at this point. Continue reading each succeeding sentence in this way.

2 Shadow Reading

Shadow Reading is a variation of Echo Reading. The teacher demonstrates how to read an entire passage fluently and then offers support and feedback to the students as they read the same passage.

- Gather together a small group and give each member the same text at their independent reading level.
- Read the entire text expressively and fluently and have the students follow along.
- Re-read the text fluently together.
- Have the students re-read as needed. Students can re-read to partners or in small groups.
- Have the students offer each other constructive feedback about the fluency of the oral reading.

3 Assisted Reading

Assisted Reading is a time for solo reading as the teacher, or a person acting as a mentor, works one-on-one with a student.

Before beginning any assisted reading, it is important that mentors, e.g. **teacher assistants, parents at home, parent volunteers in the classroom, older students, classmates** be trained in the processes. This training might include how to assist a reader when he or she selects a text, and ways to encourage and support the reader when reading.

• Have the mentor and student sit side by side. The mentor reads the text at a reasonable pace and demonstrates appropriate fluency and expression.

• Have the mentor ask the student to start reading the text alone. At any pause or stumble, the mentor can quickly supply the word or phrase. It is important to emphasise to the mentor that the decoding of individual words should not take place during this activity as this will impede fluency. Decoding of words is important and should be practised, but at another time.

• Repeat the reading as necessary. Have the mentor offer encouragement and constructive feedback to the reader.

4 Shared Reading

Shared Reading is a procedure that allows students to participate in oral reading in a supported way. The teacher reads aloud from an enlarged text and invites the students to participate in a way that makes them feel comfortable (see this book, Chapter 1 — Use of Texts, Section 1).

5 Choral Reading

Choral Reading involves students reading a text orally together with the intention of making a meaningful and enjoyable performance. Choral Reading is often an enjoyable part of the Shared Reading procedure. Although choral reading is usually associated with reading poetry, repeated dialogue or repetitive refrains, the focus is on reading the text rather than reciting it from memory.

• Select a text to read. The text should be easily accessible to all so it may be an enlarged text, an overhead transparency or chart.

• Model the reading of the text, demonstrating how to use the voice to express meaning.

• Allocate parts of the text to various groups of students.

• Read aloud together several times assisting groups to read allocated sections.

• Add any props, sound effects or movement that will enhance the presentation of the text. Encourage the students to perform the reading for an audience, e.g. **other students at the school assembly, visitors to the class, parents at an open day.**

6 Tape-assisted Reading

Tape-assisted Reading involves the students reading along with a fluent reader on an audiotape. Good quality, commercially produced tape and text sets are available. Teachers may also wish to record their own tapes as an additional support for texts currently used in the class. Parent volunteers, older students or teacher assistants can also provide models of fluent reading for these tapes. Asking students to produce text and tape sets, including personally written texts, is an excellent way to motivate students to develop fluency.

- Choose a text and a tape at an appropriate reading level (at or just above an independent level). Students listen to the tape and follow along.
- Direct students to listen to the tape again joining in where they are able.
- Have the students re-read the text while listening to the tape. Continue in this way until students can read the text fluently without the tape.

Other forms of technology such as e-books and CD-ROMs can also be used for this purpose.

7 Readers' Theatre

Readers' Theatre is an oral performance of a script. The focus is on interpreting the script rather than memorising it. Readers' Theatre is the perfect forum for readers to practise fluency through the re-reading of a text (see this book, Chapter 1— Use of Texts, Section 1).

8 Radio Reading

Radio Reading (Optiz 1998) is another supported oral reading activity where students have the opportunity to present rehearsed material to other students. While one group performs the reading, the rest of the class are the audience as they 'listen to the radio'.

- Select or have students select a text to be read. Review the text.
- Divide students into small groups. If necessary, help them select sections from the text so each member has a part to read.
- Show how to prepare their sections for oral reading. Introduce a marking key if appropriate.

Marking Key	
P — Pause	**WV** —Woman's Voice
E — Emphasise	**//** — Longer Pause
F — Show Feelings	**L** — Loud Voice
DV — Deep Voice	**W** — Whisper

Figure 1.12 Marking Key for Radio Reading

- Provide students with the opportunity to prepare their scripts for reading. Students can choose to prepare their scripts either at home or school or both.
- Ask students to rehearse their section of the text. Students work together at this point to support one another and offer suggestions. Each student also prepares open-ended questions to stimulate a short discussion about their section of the text.
- Ask one member of the radio reading group to introduce the text and the readers. Have the group commence reading.
- At the conclusion of the reading invite readers to lead a brief discussion about their section of the text.
- Provide opportunities for the audience to give feedback. A simple framework can be used such as 'It was good when _____. It was even better when _____. It was absolutely fantastic when _____.'

9 Poetry Club

A Poetry Club (Opitz 1998) provides a forum for performing poetry to an audience. Students can practise re-reading for authentic purposes. Students can perform poems, and possibly include information about the poet or their reasons for choosing a particular poem.

Before beginning a poetry club, it is important to familiarise students with poetry. This can be achieved by reading poetry, displaying poems on pin up boards in the classroom, encouraging students to borrow poetry texts from the school library or encouraging them to bring their favourite poems from home. Students will also benefit from being involved in many Modelled, Shared and Guided Reading sessions that use poems as the text.

- Ask students to select their favourite poem and give them an opportunity to rehearse it. Students can choose to work in groups, pairs or individually.
- Encourage students to try different ways of phrasing, different intonations or pace or using different voices for effect.
- Provide students with time to rehearse their poem, encouraging other students to provide constructive feedback.
- Invite students to participate in poetry club by reciting their chosen poem. This should be as non-threatening as possible to avoid students feeling pressured to perform.

10 Buddy Reading

Reading to younger 'buddies' provides an opportunity for older students to model fluent reading. Older readers, especially those who are struggling, need opportunities to read lots of 'easy' texts. These students often see reading 'easy' texts, deemed 'baby books', as unacceptable and undesirable. If these students read to younger buddies, they will feel that the texts are quite acceptable.

One teacher shares her experience using Buddy Reading.

Buddy Reading in Year Six

In my Year Six class I had students with a wide range of reading abilities. Some students were reading adult level novels while some struggled with even basic texts. Our class already had a buddy class relationship with a Year One class as the students were involved in cross-age tutoring in mathematics.

The Year One teacher and I decided to increase the contact between the two classes to:
– promote enthusiasm for reading
– provide good models of fluent oral reading
– provide authentic audiences for oral reading and writing.

The first thing we did in our reading project was to interview the Year One students to find out their interests. With this information, the Year Six students went to the school library to find a text they thought would appeal to their buddy.

Once back in the classroom, I had to think of a way to get the students to become fluent readers of the selected text. I decided to have the students come up with an activity for their buddy to do before, during and after reading. This way the Year Six students had to read the text several times to find appropriate discussion questions and activities.

Once the students had decided on their activities and rehearsed the reading of the text several times they were required to choose a peer and demonstrate their 'lesson'. Peers were required to give feedback on positive aspects or suggest possible changes.

Once we were satisfied with our reading, the class, armed with their text headed off to the buddy class. The buddy reading was successfully completed and all students were absorbed in the activity.

On returning to our classroom, we debriefed about the experience and made suggestions for future buddy reading sessions.

On subsequent visits, the Year Six students often chose texts suggested by their classmates as these texts had been a great success with other young buddies. The Year Six rehearsed for their buddies without complaint and gained a great deal from their experiences. The oral reading was fluent and expressive as the students deliberated over how different parts would be read. The success experienced in this activity by struggling readers helped them to see reading as an enjoyable activity and not a chore. The reading of 'easy' texts was legitimised and gave all students the practice they needed to improve their fluency.

SECTION 3
Promoting Reading

Reading is a complex process that is approached with different degrees of enthusiasm by each person. Some readers are less enthusiastic about choosing to read than others.

In any classroom, a teacher may identify the following students.
• Those that read well but have little interest in doing so.
• Those interested in reading but don't read well.
• Those that have no interest in reading regularly and are at risk of not coping with literacy tasks.
• Those that have specific learning problems that impede their ability and willingness to read.

The following factors may be influencing the reading abilities of the students described above.
• Prior experiences have created a negative image of reading.
• An appealing text form or author has not been discovered.
• There is a lack of purpose for reading.
• The reading process is misunderstood e.g. **thinks that reading is saying words rather than making meaning.**
• There is no time or no encouragement to read, e.g. **sport commitments, emotional trauma.**
• By using ineffective strategies, reading has become a laborious task.
• There is insufficient prior knowledge to make meaning.

When teaching reading, one of the challenges is to encourage *all* students to develop a life-long love of reading. It's important to encourage all readers to see reading as a means of satisfying a range of purposes such as enjoyment, relaxation and information gathering.

Ways to Promote Reading

This section offers some suggestions about ways to promote reading. However, ideas that work well for a particular student or for a particular year level may have little impact the following year or with another student. Teachers need to continue to try a variety of ways to promote reading and work closely with parents to inform them of the efforts being made. Teachers can select from the following ideas and suggestions.

Environment

Create an environment conducive to reading. This could be the school or classroom library area where students can sit and read without distraction. A carpet square, beanbags, big cushions, an old armchair or sofa makes this area a comfortable special place. The area can be given additional atmosphere with displays and posters advertising reading material.

Text Selection

Ensure the classroom library has a wide variety of texts representing different authors and text forms. Include literary and informational, texts related to the students' interests, texts on a variety of reading levels as well as class-created texts, paperbacks, taped stories, comics, magazines, newspapers, brochures, catalogues, interactive CD-ROMs and e-books. Enhance the students' reading development and interests by changing the texts on a regular basis.

Displays

Ensure that texts in the classroom library are displayed, advertised, sampled and easily accessible. Select a few titles and display them attractively by topic, form or author. Bright posters with catchy phrases, puppets or models related to a text will help to create interest. Change the displayed titles frequently.

Reading Time

Establish a time for independent reading when everyone (including the teacher) reads. Allow students to choose their own reading material. Be a role model for students and share your enthusiasm for reading. Talk about the reading material you enjoy.

Sharing

After Independent Reading sessions, students can share what they have been reading with the whole class, small group or partner. Make use of reading logs and reading contracts, as some readers need tangible proof of their success.

Name:		
I'VE READ THESE TEXTS!		
Title	**Date Finished**	**I liked/didn't like it**

Figure 1.13 Sample Reading Log

Reading to Students

Help students experience a wide selection of texts by reading many different text forms, authors and genres. Often, reading a text that is part of a series encourages students to read other titles in the series. Invite community members to come and read to students.

Fads

Make links to any fads that are around at the time. Try to have available copies of texts that link to the fad.

Movies and Television

Make links between reading material and movie versions or television programs. Allow students to watch the movie versions or purchase material that is written about cartoons, series or television characters. Students can compare the written and visual versions.

Electronic Versions

Consider obtaining the electronic versions of texts as some readers may be encouraged to read the accompanying text.

Poetry

Ensure a variety of poetry texts are available. Poems can often be read relatively quickly as there is less print on the page. This is appealing for some readers.

Inventories and Surveys

Distribute an interest inventory or survey at the beginning of the school year. This information can be used to select motivating reading material based on students' interests for both the classroom and school libraries. The survey could be conducted again during the year as interests may have changed.

Author Studies

Implement author studies. Have the class or a group of students read several texts by a favourite author. Learn about the author, write letters to him or her and visit the author's Internet website. Make other texts written by that author available.

Invitations

Invite an author, illustrator, publisher or librarian to the classroom to share their work.

Book Discussion Groups

Use Book Discussion Groups to provide students with opportunities to discuss a common text that has been read (see this book, Chapter 1, Section 1—Reading Procedures). For young students, the text chosen can be one that has been read aloud and discussed as a whole class on some prior occasion. If a text has already been read aloud to the students, the discussion can be more focused.

Class-created Books

Make a class book with sections devoted to favourite jokes, riddles, poems, songs and tongue twisters. Encourage students to read and find things they can add to the favourites book. Make this available when students are reading independently.

Swapping or Exchanging Texts

Develop a system that enables students to bring in reading material they would like to swap or exchange. Provide a coupon for each text brought in and students can use the coupons to select another text.

Pen Pals

Organise pen pals or email pals for students. Maintaining this relationship encourages students to read and write.

Different Audiences

Students can find reading with and to different audiences a motivating experience. Pair students with a reading partner in another year level. Students can share what they have read with their reading buddy or an older student can read to a younger student. Students may be able to read to audiences outside the school such as residents at aged-care centres.

Student Recommendations

Students can promote and recommend texts for other students to read. Students can try any of the following activities.

• Create a poster, review or PowerPoint presentation to describe a text they have read and enjoyed.

• Write reviews that are bound into a collection and available for others to read.

• Give an oral presentation to a group or class at a designated time of the day or week about a text they have read and enjoyed.

• Create a jacket cover for a text they have read and add their comments to the cover.

• Photograph students holding their favourite text. Have the students attach a summary explaining why this text was so special. Displaying these photographs will be a way to advertise the texts to other students.

• Complete a card about the text they have read. The cards correspond to the colours of traffic lights. A green card tells others to 'go for' this text, orange means the text was 'okay' and red means 'stop' not recommended. The title, author and student's name can be written on the front of the card. On the back, students can write an explanation of why the text was given that colour coding.

• Write a review on a small card and attach the card to the classroom library shelf where the text is located. Other students can quickly read the review.

Publicity Campaigns

Have students create a publicity campaign for a text or an author. They could consider posters, videos, book reviews, websites, oral and written advertisements to promote their chosen text or author.

Computers

If a student has a particular interest in a computer game encourage the reading of the manuals and magazines that help the user through these types of games. E-books and interactive CD-ROMs are also available for reading on the computer.

Class Chart

Create a class chart on which students write the titles of texts they have read and enjoyed. From this list a 'Text of the Month' can be chosen and displayed. Sometimes peer recommendations are sufficient to encourage a student to read a text they may not have previously considered.

Reading Timeline

Have students produce a timeline of their lives naming their favourite texts throughout the years. Personal pictures, texts, text covers and illustrations can be included. The displayed timelines make great advertisements, create impromptu book discussions and show students how their reading has changed over the years.

Lonely Texts

Display several texts with the banner 'The Loneliest Texts in the Class Library'. Encourage students to read and review these texts. An incentive could be offered for reading these texts. This encourages some students to read and write about texts that seldom leave the shelves.

Read with a Friend

Have multiple copies of a text available so a group of friends can read it simultaneously. This way they can discuss the text and enjoy the shared experience.

This Is Your Life

When several students have read the same text they can create a 'This Is Your Life' program for a selected character or person from the text. The introduced guests could be other characters or people from the text.

Reviews

Publish students' or teacher's reviews of texts in the school newsletter for everyone to read. This may encourage others to seek out the text and read it.

Valuing Opinions

Increase students' self-confidence by treating them as reading experts. Show students their opinion is valued, by providing opportunities for them to share.

Parents

Encourage parents to promote reading in the home. Assist parents by providing information about how to help students learn to read, how to choose reading material, the importance of reading and how to make reading fun.

Incentive Schemes

There are numerous schemes that provide incentives for students as individuals, in small groups or as a whole class. These incentive schemes reward students for the number of texts they have read.

Karate

Explain the various levels in karate and what is required to attain each level. This notion is then carried over into reading. Create belts of various colours such as yellow, orange, green, blue, red, brown and black. Assign belt levels to the number of texts read, e.g. three texts earns a yellow belt; six earns an orange belt.

Where in the World?

Give each student a copy of a world map. Each time they read a text that relates to a country in some way, have the students colour in that country. The relationship could be based on the birthplace of the author, the setting, the country that was visited in the story, the country that was the topic of the text. An incentive can be provided after a given period of time or when a specific goal is reached.

TV Versus Reading

Begin a television-reading chart for each student or the whole class. Keep a weekly record of time spent reading and time spent watching television at home. Jointly construct guidelines for earning incentives, e.g. if the class's total reading time in a week exceeds television time, a reward is given.

Read-a-thon

Conduct a class or whole school read-a-thon over a given period of time or to achieve a set target. Keep a record of the number of pages read or the total number of texts read. Update the results regularly.

Adding Details

Have students add the name of any texts they have read to a class collection of titles. Link the recording of titles to current class themes such as adding a new carriage to a train, fruit on a tree, yachts on the ocean.

Read Around a Country

Give each student a copy of a map of a country. Each time they read a page it equates to one kilometre travelled. Have students record distances travelled by mapping a route around the country. Students can be challenged to travel the greatest distance in a given period of time.

The *First Steps Reading Map of Development* Second Edition provides further suggestions for promoting reading at each phase of development.

SECTION 4

Selecting Texts for Students

Today, readers are exposed to a vast range of texts, many consisting of both print and visual features, and conveyed through a range of media. Teachers can provide opportunities for students to access a wide range of texts by incorporating these into planned learning experiences. There will be times when newspapers, magazines or the Internet will be the most appropriate source of reading material and other times when a reading series or a text book is more appropriate. Using a variety of texts will provide students with the opportunity to navigate texts using different organisational features as well as encountering a range of language features and text structures.

This section focuses on:
• Selecting Texts for the School
• Selecting Texts for Use in the Classroom
• Selecting Texts to Send Home.

Selecting Texts for the School

At the school level, decisions are made about the reading material most suitable for students. This includes material that can be used in each classroom and material that is accessible from the school library.

In addition to a school library, many schools have a separately housed collection of texts that is used as the main source of material for reading instruction in each classroom. It is important to make school-wide decisions regarding purchasing, housing, organising, maintaining, borrowing and categorising texts from this collection. Where there are large numbers of teachers, a committee can make decisions and purchases on behalf of the whole school. Students can also be surveyed to identify their preferences.

When planning the development of a school-wide reading collection, it is beneficial to approach the task strategically and acquire texts over time. Certain factors will influence decisions. They are as follows:
• the number of classrooms and students in the school
• the number of teachers who will be sharing the collection
• material already available

• financial resources available
• the different purposes that the material will be used for.

Firstly it is helpful to take an inventory of the reading material currently in the whole school. Each teacher can contribute to this inventory.

Class Inventory and Recommendations for Purchase Teacher: _____								
Texts	Titles	Copies	Text Forms	Themes	Pubn Date	Suggested Year level	Recommendation	Priority
Linking Literacy	4	3–8	Various	Space Farms Sport	2002	Year 4	Supplementary titles that have less than 8 copies so they can be used for Guided Reading	2
Read Along	92	1	70% fiction 30% non fiction	Various	2001	Year 4/5	Desperately need high-interest, low difficulty recreational reading material for less able readers	1

Figure 1.14 Class Inventory and Recommendations for Purchase

Once this information has been collated at a whole-school level, decisions can be made about the priorities for purchasing additional material. It is important to be selective in the choices. If possible, examine and review materials before a commitment is made to purchase. To help make informed decisions about purchases, invite sales representatives into the school, visit bookstores, peruse exhibits at conferences or network with other schools. If texts are available 'on approval' from a publisher, the students could give their opinions about material.

The following points may be considered when evaluating new material.

Evaluating Texts for Purchase

Target Student Group _____

- The use of these texts is:
  - ❑ instructional reading
  - ❑ recreational reading
  - ❑ functional reading.

- The content of these texts:
  - ❑ provides opportunities to teach _____
  - ❑ appeals to the target student group
  - ❑ is a good example of a particular form
  - ❑ supports a cross-curricular focus
  - ❑ provide a variety of authentic social and cultural contexts.

- The text form of these materials:
  - ❑ makes up a sufficiently wide range
  - ❑ is part of an area of need.

- The difficulty of these texts:
  - ❑ is appropriate for the target student group.

- The features of these texts that will assist the target student group include:
  - ❑ rhyme
  - ❑ rhythm
  - ❑ repetition
  - ❑ contents, index, glossary
  - ❑ illustrations (diagrams, photos, drawings)
  - ❑ natural language
  - ❑ predictability
  - ❑ a range of authors
  - ❑ authentic information
  - ❑ up-to-date information.

- The texts include the following support materials:
  - ❑ teacher's notes
  - ❑ CD-ROMs
  - ❑ audiotapes
  - ❑ videotapes
  - ❑ big books
  - ❑ small book versions.

- These texts are relatively:
  - ❑ expensive
  - ❑ well priced
  - ❑ inexpensive.

Figure 1.15 Evaluating Texts for Purchase

Storing Texts

Once texts have been purchased, deciding where and how to store the reading material collection can be an on-going concern in many schools. Issues that frequently arise include access, co-ordination between teachers and limiting the loss of material. It is important to house the material in a central location and in a way that can be easily accessed. The reading material collection could be organised by:

– reading series
– levels within the reading series
– text forms—big books, magazines could be labelled by reports, explanations
– suggested year levels.

It is valuable if someone can monitor the reading collection and keep it in order. This could be achieved in a variety of ways.

• Give one teacher responsibility for the collection, releasing them from another duty.
• Rotate responsibility for overseeing the collection such as one teacher per month.
• House the reading collection in the library.
• Make use of volunteer help.

It is also important to use a consistent, easy-to-use sign-out system so teachers are encouraged to make use of all the material available.

Guidelines for Using the School Reading Collection

• When you check out texts, please record the details in the 'borrowing book'.
• Please return the texts within 5 weeks. Be sure to return them so that other teachers can use them.
• Everyone is responsible for correctly replacing the texts when returned.
• The room will be checked at the beginning of each month.
  The schedule is:
    February—*Mrs Xavier and Mr Logan*
    March—*Miss Jackson, Mr Santeusanio*

Selecting Texts for Use in the Classroom

In the classroom there will be times when the text is selected by the teacher, by the student/s or jointly by the teacher and students

Texts selected by teachers can be made for instructional, recreational and functional purposes.

- **Recreational Reading**: These materials are based on students' interests and are read independently by students for enjoyment and meaningful reading practice.
- **Instructional Reading**: These materials comprise reading series, big books or sets of novels that are used for explicit instruction. These texts are selected to match students' reading levels.
- **Functional Reading**: These materials involve the use of reference material such as library materials, CD-ROMs, encyclopaedias and the Internet. These texts are primarily used for investigations.

Selecting Texts for Recreational Reading

It is important to provide a variety of material for students to read for recreational purposes so that reading can be seen as an enjoyable experience based on personal choice. Student input regarding this collection is also very important. This can be accomplished through the use of simple surveys conducted at the beginning and throughout the year. An Interest Survey (see Figure 1.16) could be used at the start of the school year to find out what types of materials students like to read. A Text Preference Survey (see Figure 1.17), used later in the year, will reveal any changing student interests.

INTEREST SURVEY

1 What kinds of texts do you like to read?
- ❑ Informational
- ❑ Mystery
- ❑ Science Fiction
- ❑ Adventure
- ❑ Horror
- ❑ Other

2 What is the name of your favourite text?

3 Who are your favourite authors? (List as many as you like.)

4 Name any text you have read more than once.

5 Name any text you didn't like and explain why.

6 Give the names of some texts you have at home.

7 What are your hobbies and interests?

Figure 1.16 Sample Interest Survey

Text Preference Survey

- What are the different text forms you have read so far this year?
- What has been the text form you have enjoyed reading the most?
- What has been your favourite text this year?
- Who has been your favourite author so far this year?
- Is there any particular topic that you have grown an interest in?
- What type of formats have you found yourself reading the most?

Figure 1.17 Sample Text Preference Survey

Students are often free to choose their texts for recreational purposes and benefit from being encouraged to read a wide variety. Recreational reading time in a classroom is an ideal time for the teacher to model and discuss decisions that influence text selection.

Students in any classroom will span a wide range of reading ability levels and need to know how to select texts at an appropriate level of difficulty to suit the identified purpose.

Many different criteria contribute to text difficulty including vocabulary, sentence structure and the complexity and density of ideas. Although readability measures often account for most of these factors in an attempt to 'level' texts, it is difficult to measure the match between a reader's prior knowledge and the content of a text. Global assessments of text difficulty by teachers who know the social and cultural prior knowledge of the readers are generally quicker and as accurate as the more sophisticated methods.

A common way of classifying texts, according to their difficulty, is to use the following labels — independent, instructional and frustration.

- **Independent Level** means the highest level at which a student can read easily and fluently, without assistance, with 98% to 100% accuracy in recognising words and comprehending 90% of the text. A student could read the text alone with ease.

- **Instructional Level** means the highest level at which a student can still make meaning, provided preparation and assistance is received from the teacher. Word recognition is 95% accurate with at least 80% comprehension. These texts are most appropriate for the explicit teaching of reading.

- **Frustration Level** is the level at which a student's reading strategies break down. Fluency disappears, word recognition errors are numerous, comprehension is below 70% and often signs of emotional tension, discomfort and a negative attitude to reading become apparent. This text is too hard for the reader at this time.

The 'Rule of Thumb' is a simple way that supports readers to judge text difficulty levels. When using the 'Rule of Thumb', students select a text they wish to read and turn to a page towards the beginning. The student reads the page and for each unknown word they put a finger down, in order, starting with the little fnger. If the thumb is put down before reaching the bottom of the page, the text may be too difficult at that time and the reader might like to select another text.

There will be times when students select texts below or above their independent level. Like adult readers, students will choose light, unsubstantial material or persist successfully with more complex material because the topic interests them. The key point is that students **choose** to read.

Within the classroom environment, the recreational reading material can be accessible to the students by being positioned in a reading corner or the class library. This could be a section of the room that is attractive and well organised so it is conducive to reading enjoyment. Comfortable seating such as beanbags, throw pillows and colourful displays of texts will promote reading and invite participation.

The students, with teacher support, can decide how the texts and other reading materials are organised. They could be sorted by text form, author or series. It is advisable to rotate the display on a regular basis and highlight new additions to the collection or a student's favourite book. Including students' publications as part of the collection helps to maintain interest.

Many different 'sign-out' systems for borrowing from the class collection can be used. These include any of the following.
• Have the students write the title and date in a notebook.
• Create systems that can be managed by selected student librarians.
• Have no sign-out system and rely on an honour system.

There will always be loss of some texts throughout the year due to natural wear and tear as well as those that 'just disappear'. If students are taught correct handling techniques, even paperbacks can last for a good number of years. It is advisable to have a process in place for the maintenance of the collection. Some classrooms have parent volunteers rostered to repair damaged texts.

Selecting Texts for Instructional Reading

As well as having a wide variety of material for students to read for recreational purposes, a classroom needs to have a supply of material, selected by the teacher, to be used for instructional purposes. The selection of this material will be closely linked to the Major Teaching Emphases on the *First Steps Map of Development Second Edition*. A variety of texts at different levels of difficulty will be required for whole class, small groups and individual instruction. The following table (see Figure 1.18) illustrates how a teacher has used the Major Teaching Emphases as a basis for making decisions about text selection.

Linking Text Selection to *First Steps Map of Development Second Edition* Major Teaching Emphases and Reading Procedures				
Reading Phase	**Substrand**	**Major Teaching Emphases**	**Reading Procedure**	**Text Selected**
Experimental	Use of Texts	Read and re-read a variety of texts both literary and informational	Reading to students (whole class)	A poster of a song or poem the students have learnt.
Experimental	Contextual Understanding	Draw students' attention to the ways people or characters are represented in texts and discuss alternatives	Shared Reading (whole class)	A Big Book copy of a text such as *The Paper Bag Princess* by R. Munsch which represents fairytale characters in different ways.
Experimental	Conventions	Build students' knowledge about different text forms, e.g. purpose, structure and organisation	Guided Reading (6 students in a group)	Seven copies of *First, Take the Flour ...* by Isabel Bissett
Experimental	Processes and Strategies	Consolidate known comprehension strategies and teach additional strategies, e.g. connecting	Modelled Reading	*Wanda-Linda Goes Berserk* by Kaz Cooke

Figure 1.18 Linking Text Selection to *First Steps Map of Development Second Edition*

Reading material that is used for instructional purposes needs to be easily accessible for the teacher. These materials need not be accessible to students prior to their use. Teachers may wish to use some materials 'sight unseen' for the purpose of prediction and maintaining interest. After students have been exposed to the materials in instructional lessons, it can be useful to have them available for on-going reading and revisiting.

Selecting Texts for Functional Reading

Functional reading occurs when students access texts such as websites, encyclopaedias, subject specific texts and CD-ROMs in order to gather information for a particular purpose. Investigations in health education, science and studies of society and environment often require students to gather information from a variety of sources and present it in some way, e.g. **report, speech or PowerPoint presentation**. It is important to encourage students to access material available from sources outside the school such as the community library and home environment.

Materials for functional reading may not be housed in the classroom on a permanent basis. Often the rich source of this material is the school library. Schools use a variety of systems to allow students access to library resources. In addition, at various times throughout the year, teachers might organise a bulk loan of material relevant to a particular topic that is kept in the classroom for an extended period of time.

Selecting Texts to Send Home

Texts taken home are used to help develop a love of reading and practise those reading strategies that are being taught. Reading at home can assist and accelerate the acquisition of reading strategies, improve vocabulary and comprehension, and help develop automaticity and fluency.

There are times when the home-reading material will be chosen by the teacher and other times when the students will make their selections. Students can be encouraged to use the 'Rule of Thumb' method to guide their selections. There will be times when students select texts that are too easy or too difficult for them. It is essential to communicate to parents your awareness of students' self-selected texts and share the most appropriate home-reading experience for the student with that text. One way to communicate this easily to the parents is through the use of different coloured tags.

For example,
- A red tag indicates that the student should be able to read the text independently.
- A blue tag indicates that the student will need support to read the text.
- A green tag indicates the text is best read to the student.

The amount of time spent on home reading and the way it is organised will vary. With younger students, more direction may be necessary and the teacher may select the text that is read. A recording of the texts can be kept and the parents can be asked to sign the entry to indicate that the reading occurred. With older students, selection of material and choice about how much is to be read could be individual decisions. Older students can also keep a record of the material that they read. Teachers can create guidelines as to how much time should be spent reading each week but allow flexibility as to how this occurs.

Helping Parents Understand Home Reading

With any reading that occurs at home, the key is clear communication between the teacher and the parents so that students develop a life-long love of reading. Newsletters, emails and parent information sessions at the beginning of the school year are effective ways of informing parents about guidelines and the outcomes of reading at home.

It is also important to alert parents to the variety of ways of providing opportunities for students to read at home. Students will benefit from reading at home in any of the following ways.
- Read aloud to a parent, sibling or other relation.
- Read silently and discuss with a parent — discussion could be about the content of the text, reactions to the text, difficulties experienced, strategies used, visual images created, links to other reading material.
- Read silently with no questions asked — this is quite common for adult readers so students should be allowed to do the same.
- Read along with a parent, sibling or other relation.
- Listen to a text read aloud.

It is important to inform parents how they can make oral reading a positive experience for students in the home setting. A parent card that will provide parents with information about supporting oral reading is available on the CD-ROM.

Supporting Oral Reading at Home

If your child makes a mistake and corrects the error ...	If your child comes to a word they don't know and pauses ...	If your child makes a mistake which does not make sense ...	If your child makes a mistake which does make sense ...
• Offer praise or support for making the correction.	• Wait and give them time to work it out. • If they're successful, encourage them to read on to maintain meaning. • If they are likely to know the word, ask them to go back to the beginning of the sentence and have another go at it. • Ask them to guess a word which begins with the same letter and would make sense. • Ask a question which will give a clue to the meaning e.g. *"How do you think Johnny feels? Angry?"* • If they are unlikely to know the word, say it quickly and encourage them to keep reading to maintain fluency and avoid loss of meaning.	• Wait to see if they work it out for themselves and offer praise if they do. • If they don't correct the word themselves ask, *"Does that make sense?"* • Ask a question which will give a clue to what the word is e.g. *"Where will he go to catch the train?"* • If they are unlikely to know the word, say it quickly and encourage the child to read on. Later, when the whole text has been read, go back to unknown words and help your child use other word identification strategies such as: – sounding out individual sounds in a word – sounding out chunks of words, e.g. *base or root of the word, prefixes and suffixes* – looking at the words around it.	• Do nothing until the child has finished. • When they have finished, go back to the word and say *"You said this word was ——; it made sense but it begins (or ends) with the letter — so what do you think it could be?"* • You may wish to discuss the letters of the word with your child and see if they can think of any other words with similar letters.

Figure 1.19 Supporting Oral Reading at Home

CHAPTER 2

Contextual Understanding

Overview

The Contextual Understanding substrand focuses on how the interpretation, choice of language and the shaping of a text vary according to the context in which it is used. From an early age, children know that the language used in the playground may not be as appropriate or effective in another context. Several factors influence the use of language.

- Purpose of communication
- Subject matter
- Mode of communication (spoken, written, visual)
- Roles and relationships between the participants
- Social situation

It is important that students are provided with opportunities to reflect on how language varies and needs to be amended according to purpose, subject, mode of communication and roles.

Included in this chapter is Section 1—Developing Contextual Understanding.

Figure 2.1

Developing Contextual Understanding

Refuse to be put in a basket

The two different readings and two different meanings of the above sign depend on where the reader places the emphasis in the first word. This sign exemplifies the role of contextual understanding in language. If the reader assumes REFUSE to be trash or rubbish, it could be assumed that the sign is a command or a direction from an authority in a particular place such as a school or public park. If the reader assumes REFUSE to mean 'decline', then the sign takes on a more abstract, deeper meaning about not conforming with mainstream beliefs. The sign may be found on a bumper sticker or as a T-shirt slogan.

Much hinges on where the sign is located, who put it there and the relationship between the writer and the reader. The collective situational aspects of the reading, and the social and cultural perceptions of the writer and the reader, make up what is known as contextual understanding.

Contextual Understanding and Critical Literacy

Contextual Understanding is an awareness of how the context affects the interpretation and choice of language. From an early age, children become aware that the spoken language varies according to the situation in which it is used. Children often receive timely feedback about what they have said and how they have said it. However, the development of contextual understanding by a reader is often less overt and requires explicit teaching. Students need to be aware, for example, that an advertisement on a website is aimed at persuading them to buy something and will use a number of devices to influence them.

Critical literacy is an approach to literacy that involves analysing and questioning texts to reveal the beliefs and values behind the surface meanings, and to see how a reader can be influenced and affected. By interrogating texts, readers become aware of how language is used to position particular social and cultural groups and practices, often preserving relationships of power. For example, a reader may question an historical account of land settlement that leaves out or understates the importance of an indigenous population. Because critical literacy can challenge existing power relationships and social practices, it is inevitably political, so teachers need to reflect regularly on what constitutes critical literacy in the classroom, and its impact on the school community.

To be critically literate, students need to know how context affects the interpretation of language. Having an understanding of situational and socio-cultural contexts equips a reader with the fundamental knowledge to deconstruct, analyse and interrogate texts. Although Contextual Understanding and critical literacy are not synonymous, teaching students to be aware of the relationship between context and the interpretation of language provides a sound foundation for critical literacy approaches.

Contextual Understanding and Reading

To become effective readers, students need to become aware of the ways the author or illustrator has used devices for various effects in the text and how this influences them as readers. Readers need to be taught about situational context and socio-cultural context, including how their own view of the world leads them to make an interpretation of a text. Students need to understand how and why their interpretation may differ from the interpretation of others.

Even the simplest texts carry messages of various kinds, that reflect the background, biases and culture of the author and illustrator.

Situational Context

An author's choice of language can vary according to the context in which it is used. Several factors influence this choice of language:
• the author's purpose of communication
• subject matter
• the text type—report, email, formal letter
• the roles and relationships between the communicating participants—memo from a company director to the employees, memo from one colleague to another.

Changing any of these factors may have an impact on the language being used.

The same factors influence how a reader uses and interprets text. The reader is influenced by:
• the purpose for reading
• their knowledge and familiarity with the topic or subject

- the situation in which the reading takes place
- the relationship between the author and the reader.

Socio-cultural Context

These are broader influences that have an impact on language usage. All texts reflect, to some extent, the expectations and values of the social and cultural groups of the time they were written. This understanding of socio-cultural context involves knowing that:

- the way people use language both reflects and shapes their socio-cultural outlook—the beliefs, values and assumptions of their socio-cultural group, especially with regard to gender, ethnicity and status
- texts will be interpreted differently by different people according to their socio-cultural background—awareness of the influence of socio-cultural factors on composing and comprehending texts is pivotal
- language and culture are strongly related
- language is intentionally crafted, communicated and manipulated to influence others, often to maintain or challenge existing power relationships between groups like employers and employees, businesses and consumers, and governments and citizens
- various forms of English are used around the world that reflect and shape socio-cultural attitudes and assumptions, including variations of standard English generally used in formal communication, education and some professional settings.

When an author writes a text, his or her socio-cultural context will influence the type of language he or she uses. Likewise the moment a text is picked up by a reader, the reader's view of the world, society and culture will influence their reading and interpretation of the text. Texts are not neutral. Each reader will have a different reading of the text according to what he or she brings to that text. For example, an environmentalist and a mining engineer might react very differently to a report on Antarctica as each person reads the text with a different set of values, beliefs and understanding about the topic.

Why Teach Contextual Understanding?

The world today is swamped with information from a range of media and a variety of sources. Developing contextual understanding allows students to analyse this information and:

- become aware that texts are open to several valid interpretations
- monitor, evaluate and reaffirm their understandings of texts
- recognise the 'power' of texts and how they can be influential in positioning readers.

- recognise and evaluate the beliefs that influence texts
- make informed decisions about their view on specific topics
- become aware that language is constructed, used and manipulated in powerful ways.

A wide variety of materials is necessary for teaching contextual understanding. Authentic reading materials such as magazines, advertising brochures, food packaging and newspapers often reveal more about the beliefs, values and assumptions of the authors than school books. However, old reading series that are often deemed 'politically incorrect' and fairy tales are worth interrogating as they reflect the values of times and circumstances that contrast with modern, dominant social norms.

What Students Need to Know

If students are going to be able to offer opinions and justify and substantiate those opinions, they need to be aware of the following.
- Authors and illustrators present a view of the world that can be challenged.
- Authors and illustrators represent facts, events, characters and people in different ways.
- Authors and illustrators use devices to achieve a specific purpose.

Authors and illustrators present a view of the world that can be challenged.

- Texts can be looked at from various points of view.
- Texts are selective versions of reality, told from a particular point of view.
- There is no one right interpretation of a text. It is possible to challenge and resist the preferred or dominant reading and the way people, places and events are depicted.
- Authors write for a particular audience and assume that audiences have specific cultural knowledge and values.
- The values of a dominant group or culture are often represented as the norm.
- There are gaps and silences in every text. Readers will fill these gaps differently based on their own socio-cultural context.

Authors and illustrators represent facts, events, characters and people in different ways.

- Facts and events are chosen or omitted and then represented by authors and illustrators to present a particular point of view.
- Characters from literary texts are not real but are constructed by authors and illustrators to create a particular representation.

- When creating informational texts, authors select information to represent people in a certain way.

Consider the following representations.

Text Excerpt	What Does This Say About...?
Often the class would have parties where the girls would bring something they had cooked, and the boys brought the drinks.	Gender
Day after day, Grandma sat in her chair, rocking back and forth, unaware of most of what was happening around her.	Age
The librarian peered over the top of her spectacles, shook her bob of greying hair, and narrowed her eyes.	Occupation
Everyone except Jake went to see the show. His dad had spent the house-keeping money on a horse race.	Socio-economic status
Each captain took turns to pick kids for their teams until only the skinny kids with glasses remained.	Physical appearance
We asked Phuong to join our group because we wanted someone who was good at mathematics.	Cultural background
The farmer was confused by the modern escalator.	Geographical background

Figure 2.2 Representations

Authors and illustrators use devices to achieve a specific purpose.

Devices Used by Authors

Authors use language devices to influence the reader. The author's use of language devices often reveals their socio-cultural background. To comprehend a text and interpret the author's message, a reader needs to understand the socio-cultural perspective from which a text is written.

Authors also choose language devices that suit the situational context of the language event, e.g. **purpose, subject matter, relationship between the author and the reader.**

Consider the following devices used by authors.

Analogy

Using analogy involves the comparison of one thing with another, sometimes extending the comparison too far in seeking to persuade, e.g. **A classroom is just like an extended family, so every student deserves the sort of care and affection they would receive from their parents.**

Bribery

This is a persuasive device commonly used in advertising. Bonuses, free products, discounts and privileges are offered to the reader, e.g. **Buy one packet—get one packet free.**

Connotation

Connotation refers to the suggestion of a meaning by a word beyond what it explicitly denotes or describes. The suggestion can create positive or negative influences.

Millionaire Sophie Enwright had a reputation for being **thrifty.**
Millionaire Sophie Enwright had a reputation for being **stingy.**
Millionaire Sophie Enwright had a reputation for being **frugal.**
Millionaire Sophie Enwright had a reputation for being **penny-wise.**

Euphemism

News articles often use a euphemism or a mild expression in place of a blunt one. For example, the word **eliminate** will be used instead of **kill**, when describing the actions of a nation's army.

Exaggeration

This involves the use of sweeping statements, e.g. **Prefects had the power of life and death over junior boys.**

Figurative language

Figurative language refers to using language not meant to be read literally. These include similes (e.g. **cute as a button**), metaphors (e.g. **he was a lion in battle**), idioms (e.g. **it's raining cats and dogs**) and hyperbole (e.g. **I could eat a horse**). The understanding of figurative language is determined by a shared socio-cultural context.

Flattery

Flattery (particularly in advertising) involves an appeal to the reader's self image, including the need to belong or the need for prestige, e.g. **Any intelligent person knows...** Flattery also includes association — discrediting or enhancing a position by association with some other person, group or idea, e.g. **You must be joking about secret ballots for trade unions. I expect that sort of comment from a communist.**

Flashback

This is a device commonly used in literary texts that explores events that have occurred previously and have had an impact on the current situation. Flashback is often achieved through dream sequences, reflecting on memories or the narration of one of the characters. Flashback may be used to create a sense of nostalgia or illustrate selective recall.

Foreshadowing

Foreshadowing is a device commonly used in literary texts to hint at what is to come. For example, advertisers use foreshadowing by showing a preview of an advertisement in one television break and the entire advertisement in the next break.

Inclusion of details

The author has selected only those details that support his or her perspective. Other details that would contradict the perspective have been omitted.

Irony, wit and humour

Irony, wit and humour are devices that rely heavily on a shared socio-cultural context to achieve the author's purpose.

Irony uses a contrast between the reality and the expectation, what is said and what is meant or what appears to be true and what is true, e.g. **As he watched the rain fall, Peter remarked, "Lovely day for a picnic".**

Wit refers to the perception and expression of a relationship between seemingly incompatible or different things in a cleverly amusing way.

Humour is the perception, enjoyment or expression of something that is amusing, comical, incongruous or absurd.

Irrelevance

Irrelevance is including points or arguments that do not contribute to the main idea, with the aim of distracting the reader.

Omission of details

The author has omitted the fact that Jones' two major rivals had been injured and were unable to compete.

> ### Jones Blitzes Field
>
> The brilliant Archie Jones yesterday emphasised his dominance over other sprinters in the south-west region when he won the Regional 100-metre Summer Sprint. Jones led from start to finish, leaving his opponents trailing in his wake.

Figure 2.3 Jones Blitzes Field

Overgeneralisation

This is the use of a statement that encompasses a wide group of people or situations and is not based on fact, e.g. **Everyone knows that … dogs are smarter than cats.**

Oversimplification

This occurs when a simple (and often single) statement is used to explain a situation that is the result of a number of complex and interwoven factors, e.g. **The Allies won World War II because of their ascendancy in the air.**

Personification

Personification means to give human qualities to inanimate objects and abstract ideas, e.g. **The XYZ Company believes....., The stuffed bear smiled as he was lifted from the ground.**

Personalisation

This involves adopting a tone of intimacy through the use of personal pronouns, e.g. **We were attacked because of who we are and what we believe.** It can include commands, e.g. **Your country needs you!** and rhetorical questions, e.g. **Are you getting a fair deal at work?**

Print size and font selection

Choosing specific words to be printed in bold type, italics, colour or in a larger font size can indicate aspects the author feels are important for the reader to notice. Different fonts can be used for different reasons. A handwriting font, for instance, may be used to suggest a familiar or informal relationship between the author and reader.

Quoting someone out of context

Quoting someone out of context to mislead or influence the reader can create bias. Authors often select a particular section of a written or spoken text and can use this section to present a different impression or point of view.

Repeating words or phrases

Repetition is used to persuade readers by emphasising particular parts of a text, e.g. **The company has offered no support to the community. Nil. None. Zilch.**

Symbolism

A symbol is anything that can be used to represent something else, e.g. dressing a character in black, the sound of a small stream.

To understand the symbols used in text the reader needs to share a similar cultural background to the author. Symbols are often culturally specific and the same meaning may not necessarily be understood between cultures, e.g. the colour white is associated with weddings in Australia but with funerals in Bali.

Sarcasm and satire

Sarcasm and satire rely heavily on a shared socio-cultural context to achieve the author's purpose. Sarcasm is scathing language that is intended to offend or ridicule.

Satire ridicules human weaknesses, vices or follies with the intention of bringing about social reform.

Testimony

The use of quotations from experts or people positively associated with a situation or product is called testimony. Testimony also includes the use of statistics, e.g. Nine out of ten dentists agree that ...

Understatement

Understatement is used when trying to downplay the gravity of a situation or event, e.g. In the recent floods, several lives were lost. (Actually the death toll was close to twenty.)

Devices Used by Illustrators

Illustrators use visual devices to try to influence the reader. Consider the following devices used by illustrators.

Amount of detail

Illustrators include varying amounts of details to enhance and complement the text. In a single picture, details can convey information that would take an author many sentences. Details also tend to give a more realistic feel to the illustrations.

Artistic style

The artistic style refers to the way the illustrations are rendered. The artistic style may tend towards realistic or towards representational. In realistic art, subjects and objects are portrayed with detailed accuracy, as they would be in real life. On the other hand, in representational art, the illustrator has made no attempt to make the art appear realistic. Each artistic style conveys a different message to the reader.

Colour

Colours have symbolic meaning. Illustrators often choose colours to create certain effects, e.g. **strong bold colours may indicate happiness, dark sombre colours may indicate night.**

Composition and page design

The placement of visual elements on a page or in a text is another device illustrators use. Objects placed in the foreground tend to have more prominence than those in the background. Visual elements placed on the right-hand page have prominence over those on the left. Newspapers exploit this prominence by increasing the cost of advertisements in that section of the page. An illustrator or book designer can also attract the reader's attention through the use of white spaces in the page design.

Medium

Medium refers to the material or technique an illustrator has used, e.g. **collage, charcoal, watercolours, photographs.** The choice of medium by the illustrator can provide readers with clues about the message or purpose of the text, e.g. **photographs suggest the text is realistic.**

Size

Illustrators may indicate the more important characters or people by making them larger than others. The relative sizes of visual elements may also change at different places in a text as different points are emphasised.

Supporting the Development of Contextual Understanding

Contextual Understanding is an integral part of a comprehensive approach to teaching reading. It is best taught within the context of established reading procedures.

Modelled Reading provides an ideal forum for the teacher to think aloud to demonstrate how the text is being interrogated during the reading.

Shared Reading enables the students and the teacher to question the text and the author's motives together, jointly constructing meaning.

Guided Reading is a forum for students to work almost independently, using a teacher-provided scaffold to pose revealing questions at pre-determined checkpoints.

Effective teaching and learning practices can also provide a springboard for supporting the development of contextual understanding.

These effective teaching and learning practices include:
- Familiarising
- Discussing
- Analysing
- Investigating
- Innovating
- Simulating
- Reflecting

Familiarising involves bringing different texts and different aspects of texts to the attention of students. Material such as greeting cards, cereal packets and magazine advertisements can be collected, compared, displayed, and most importantly, discussed.

Discussing is central to helping students become text analysts. Initially teachers may stimulate discussion by posing critical questions about gender stereotypes in folk and fairy tales or persuasive devices in junk mail advertisements or magazine articles. A scan of the cover of a book may lead to a question about the intended audience or whether the text appears to be literary or informational. In time, students can interrogate texts alone, posing many of the questions listed later in this chapter.

Prediction and confirmation are additional important aspects to be discussed. By discussing these aspects students may then be able to detect familiar patterns of dominant cultural values in texts.

Analysing texts involves examining parts of the text to reveal the social and cultural values that are embedded in them. This analysis is often accomplished by comparing similar texts.
Consider the following.

- Compare two versions of the same story, same event or same phenomenon.
- Compare the way characters or groups of people are portrayed in different texts.
- Compare the characters, setting or plot of two literary texts.
- Compare the points of view, accuracy, validity and currency of 'factual' accounts. Include a comparison of the perspectives adopted by the media in different parts of the world and different interest groups.

Analysing parts of a text can also mean identifying devices that an author or illustrator has used. This may include finding examples of bias, exaggeration in text or the use of colour in illustrations or photographs.

Investigating a text can encompass finding out, analysing and questioning who has written the text, when, for what purpose and how the author or illustrator has chosen to convey the message. This might include investigating who owns a magazine or sponsors a website, whether the author has credibility in the field or the target audience of the text.

Innovating by amending an existing text or transforming a text by re-creating it in another genre, form, mode, medium or format enables students to disrupt the reading of a text. Students are able to deconstruct and reconstruct parts of a text to reveal different perspectives. Several fairytales have already been the subject of innovations, changing gender roles or altering the time or place. Simpler innovations could involve substituting alternative words for those with excessively positive or negative connotations. Innovation can also incorporate removing parts of a text, or adding parts such as a sequel or postscript.

Simulating involves assuming the role of another person or group of people to interpret a text from a different viewpoint. The point of view may differ on the basis of culture, time, geography, age, gender or other factors. Some books are based on varied perspectives, such as *The Town Mouse and The Country Mouse*, and provide insights into two alternative points of view.

Reflecting can be accomplished by promoting discussion about the different identities students may assume when reading a text. Students may, at different times, see themselves as a sister, a daughter, a supporter of the nation, a supporter of the state or province, a conservationist, a youth, a member of a cultural or religious group. Similarly, students can reflect on the divided loyalties that characters in texts may experience when they confront situations from their different identities.

Reflecting also involves the consideration of personal values that underpin students' responses to texts. When responses to reading are elaborated and substantiated, students can reflect on how their thinking is driven by their experiences, beliefs and attitudes.

Generic Questions for Discussing Texts

Teachers can use the following lists to choose and frame questions that will stimulate discussion according to the needs of their students, the text selected and the purpose of the session. When answering these questions, students can be expected to substantiate, justify and extend their answers. It may be necessary to ask further questions such as:

Q: From whose point of view is the text written?
A: From an adult's point of view
Q: Why do you think that? or How do you know?

What? (the subject matter)
- What is the text about?
- What type of text is this?
- What do you think the text means?
- What do others think the text means?
- What and who is included or left out?
- What and who is valued or devalued?

Figure 2.4a

Why? (purpose)
- Why was it written?

Figure 2.4b

When?
- When was it written?

Figure 2.4c

Who? (the relationship between author and reader)
- Who wrote the text?
- What do you know about the author?
- Who was the text written for?
- From whose point of view is the text written?
- How does your socio-cultural context (values) affect your interpretation of the text?

Figure 2.4d

How? (style and tone of communication)
- How does the author create his or her effect?
- How could it have been written differently, e.g. *different genre, form, mode, medium, format*
- How does this text compare with similar texts that you have read?

Figure 2.4e

CHAPTER 3
Conventions

Overview

The Conventions substrand focuses on the knowledge of the structures and features of a variety of texts. Students today need to be aware of the language structures and features that are typical of standard English so they are able to communicate successfully in formal settings. This knowledge empowers students to make choices about the mode of communication, the type of text, the grammatical structures, the presentation style and the words that are most appropriate and effective in a particular setting. They are able to talk about the choices they have made and the language structures and features they can recognise in their daily encounters with language. For example, students preparing a recount of a school event for a local newspaper may decide (after reading several newspaper articles) that they need to use a particular text structure and its grammatical conventions to meet the expectations of the newspaper's readers.

This chapter includes information on developing students' knowledge and understandings of conventions. The four sections are as follows:
• Section 1—Developing Phonological Awareness
• Section 2—Teaching Graphophonics
• Section 3—Vocabulary Knowledge
• Section 4—Text Form Knowledge.

Figure 3.1

Effective Teaching of Conventions

The long-term goal for all students is that they can use conventions correctly and independently during the reading or writing of authentic texts. An analytic approach where students 'discover' these conventions works best for engaging students in meaningful teaching and learning.

The following reflects the teaching and learning beliefs underpinning *First Steps*. It can be used as an effective teaching plan of all conventions outlined in this chapter.

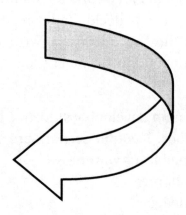

- **Select the Focus**
- **Choose the Context and the Text**

- **Assess Prior Knowledge**

- **Monitor and Provide Feedback**
- **Encourage Self-reflection**

- **Analyse and Investigate,**
- **Represent or Capture Learning**

- **Provide Guided Practice Activities**

- **Encourage Independent Application**

Figure 3.2 Effective Teaching of Conventions

Assess Prior Knowledge

Assessment is an ongoing process of data collection and evaluation. When assessing students' knowledge of conventions, it is suggested that data be collected in the context of classroom literacy events. These may include any of the following:

• observing students in the act of reading and writing
• analysing work products
• involving the student in conversations, e.g. **interviews, conferences, questionnaires.**

Whichever method is used to collect data, it is important that teaching decisions are based on an analysis of students' strengths and areas of need.

Select the Focus and Choose the Context and the Text

When selecting conventions for explicit teaching, consider the needs of the students, their phase of development and any curriculum requirements.

Once a focus has been selected, it is necessary to choose an appropriate context and text. These may include teacher-selected texts, teacher written texts, students' written or transcribed texts or environmental print.

Analyse and Investigate, Represent or Capture Learning

Analysing involves the students in problem solving, evaluating and classifying as they investigate the parts to understand its relationship to the whole and how each part works. Investigating may involve students looking at letters or combinations of letters in words, looking at words in the context of a sentence or paragraph, listening for individual phonemes in words or analysing paragraphs within texts.

If it is appropriate, the understandings learnt can be represented or captured in some way. This may include developing a chart, making a journal entry or creating a display.

Provide Guided Practice Activities

Guided Practice Activities involve the teacher structuring learning experiences that provide students with support and scaffolds, as they practise their growing understandings.

Students can be provided with practice activities such as:

• locating words containing a focus letter or letter combinations
• matching words written on cards to those in the text

- sorting words in a variety of ways
- producing rhyming words
- finding words to fit a given criterion
- identifying patterns in a text.

The *First Steps Reading Map of Development Second Edition*, provides phase-specific, guided practice activities.

Encourage Independent Application

Once time has been spent explicitly teaching conventions, teachers can provide opportunities for this knowledge to be transferred to other subject areas.

Monitor and Provide Feedback and Encourage Self-reflection

On-going monitoring will ensure that learning experiences are appropriate for the developing understandings of students.

The provision of explicit feedback is crucial to students if they are to refine, reshape and enhance their understandings of conventions. It is important that feedback be directed at the strategies or understandings students are using or attempting to use.

Encourage students to reflect on and record their growing understandings about conventions.

SECTION 1

Developing Phonological Awareness

What Is Phonological Awareness?

Phonological awareness is an ability to recognise, combine and manipulate the different sound units of spoken words. The minimal unit of sound in speech is called a phoneme, thus the labels phonemic awareness and phonological awareness are often used synonymously. Phonological awareness is the umbrella term that includes units of sound larger than the phoneme, such as syllables or onsets and rimes. Neither label should be confused with graphophonics, which involves the use of letters [f. Gk *graphe*— writing].

Differences between Phonological Awareness and Graphophonics	
Phonological Awareness is: • auditory • based on speech • focused on sounds.	**Graphophonics is:** • visual and auditory • based on print • focused on letters representing sounds.

Figure 3.3 Differences between Phonological Awareness and Graphophonics

Developing phonological awareness is an appropriate precursor to building a solid understanding of graphophonic relationships (Juel, Griffith and Gough, 1986). Phonological awareness is the ability to hear the abstract units of sound in speech. Consider the following tasks, all of which focus on sound, as opposed to the sound/letter relationship.

• How many words can you hear in this sentence?
  ("Jack is late for school.")
• Do these two words rhyme? (dog and log)
• Can you say 'cat' without the 'c'?
• Does 'fox' start with the same sound as 'fish'?
• What are the three sounds in the spoken word 'sat'?

Most young students can segment words into syllables, but segmenting a word into its smallest possible unit of sound, phonemes, is more difficult. Phonemes are not pronounced individually when spoken as words, but in a blended way. Phonemes are abstract. They carry no meaning, and do not sound the same in isolation as they do in context. For example, when the word 'big' is segmented, it sounds like 'buh – /i/ – guh'; extra 'schwa' sounds is introduced (buh, guh), even though these do not exist in the spoken word. Students also commonly blend words together because they do not perceive them as being separate, e.g. **'smornig' (this morning), 'havta' (have to), 'afanowu' (half an hour)**.

Students learning English as an Additional Language (EAL) often have difficulty identifying phonemes in English words, particularly where their first language does not include similar phonemes, or is not alphabetic.

Many students will develop phonological awareness through language experiences both at home and at school. Those students who have played with words when learning rhymes, songs and riddles will have had more opportunities to hear the sounds in words. However, some students will not have encountered these language experiences in the home so they may not be aware of phonemes in words. The teaching of phonological awareness should be part of a comprehensive literacy approach.

Research indicates that phonological awareness in young students is one part of effective reading instruction and is highly predictive of reading and spelling success (Stanovich 1986, 1993; Share and Stanovich 1995). Phonological awareness is an important factor but is not sufficient in and of itself to guarantee reading success (Lyon 1997). While phonological awareness should be an essential part of reading instruction, it is important that it does not dominate the reading program.

Recent studies indicate that the teaching of phonological awareness is most successful when there is an explicit focus on recognising and manipulating sound units. This research also found that instruction was often enhanced by the inclusion of print (Ehri 1998; Treiman 1993).

What Students Need to Know

The main understandings to be developed in relation to phonological awareness are as follows:
• Word Awareness, e.g. **spoken language is made up of words; words are representations of objects (cat), emotions (love) and concepts (height); words can rhyme**

- Syllable Awareness, e.g. some words have a single syllable and others have more than one
- Onset and Rime Awareness, e.g. single syllable words are made up of onsets and rimes
- Phonemic Awareness, e.g. words are made up of individual sounds or phonemes.

There is no evidence to suggest that all students acquire phonological awareness in a particular developmental sequence. However, there seems to be agreement that some elements of phonological awareness appear to be more difficult than others (Stahl and Murray 1994; Stanovich, Cunningham and Cramer 1984). For example, students are able to split words into, and manipulate, onsets and rimes more easily than individual phonemes (Fox and Routh 1975; Goswami 1994; Treiman 1992).

The table (Figure 3.4) summarises the phonological elements and the levels of difficulty within each element. When planning for teaching phonological awareness, both the elements and the level of difficulty within each element need to be considered. For instance,

Phonological Elements and Levels of Difficulty			
Element	**Easier** ——————————————————→ **More Difficult**		
Size of the Phonological Unit	word awareness	syllable awareness	onset and rime awareness	phonemic awareness
Phoneme Position	initial	final	medial
Number of Phonemes	1–3 phonemes	more than 3 phonemes	
Phonological Properties	continuants, e.g. /m/, /r/, /f/	stop sounds, e.g. /t/, /d/, /p/	
Phonological Dimension	isolating	blending	segmenting	manipulating
Phonological Task (illustrated with rhyming)	identifying "Does dog rhyme with log?"	matching "Which one rhymes with dog? (cat, log)	oddity "Which one doesn't rhyme: toy, cat, boy?"	producing "Give me a word that rhymes with dog?"

Figure 3.4 Phonological Elements and Levels of Difficulty (adapted from Smith, Simmons and Kame'enui 1995)

when students are asked to identify individual phonemes, they find it easier to identify the initial phoneme than the final or medial phoneme. Similarly, the table indicates that identifying the initial phoneme of a word is an easier task than producing a word with a given phoneme.

Supporting the Development of Phonological Awareness

The *First Steps Reading Map of Development Second Edition* provides suggestions for appropriate learning experiences for supporting students' phonological awareness in the Role Play, Experimental and Early Phases of development.

Below are further suggestions for developing phonological awareness.

Developing Word Awareness

Concept of a Word

- Discuss and name familiar objects in the environment, identifying each as a 'word', e.g. **"That's a table, 'table' is a word." "Tell me the words for some of the things you can see in the room."**
- Display the students' names on a chart at eye level and frequently refer to the names as words.
- Read a sentence from a current familiar text or rhyme and have the student put a counter into a container for each word they hear. e.g. **Humpty Dumpty sat on a wall.**

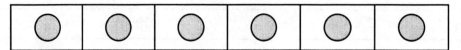

Figure 3.5

- Point to a line of print from a familiar text and have students clap each word they hear.
- As a familiar poem or rhyme is chanted, students can clap as they say each word.
- After reading a text, involve the students in oral cloze activities and have them supply the missing words.

Adding Print

- Write some words from a familiar text onto pieces of card. Distribute the cards to the students and have them find the word in the text.
- When using a big book in Modelled or Shared Reading sessions, point to the words as they are read. Encourage students to join in on subsequent readings while continuing to point to the words.

- Draw students' attention to words in a text by isolating the words in some way.
- Copy sentences from a current text onto strips of card. Have students place a coloured block on each word and then count the words.
- Write words from a familiar text or student's names onto card. Have students sort the cards into long or short words. Talk about what makes the words long or short. Have students find other short or long words.
- Copy a sentence from a familiar text on to a strip of card and have students cut the sentence into individual words. Have the students reassemble the sentence in a pocket chart (referring to the original if necessary), making sure to leave a space between the words. Ask the students to count the words in the sentence.

Developing an Awareness of Rhyming Words (identifying, matching, oddity and producing tasks)

The ability to recognise and generate rhyme is crucial to phonological awareness. Being able to recognise rhyme emerges before being able to generate rhymes.

- Read aloud from a wide range of literature featuring rhyme, rhythm and repetition.
- Read aloud from a wide range of literature featuring word play such as alliteration or substitution.
- Jointly create innovations on favourite rhymes by changing the rhyming words, e.g. **Humpty Dumpty sat on a rock. Humpty Dumpty had a big shock.**
- After reading or re-reading a rhyming text, select words from the text and have students suggest other rhyming words or alliterative words. Accept nonsense words but label them as such.
- Have students play Physical Rhyme Matching. Deal out a picture card to each student. Students must then find their partner to make a rhyming pair. Ensure students repeat the rhyming pair to reinforce the verbal production of rhymed words.
- When reading or re-reading familiar rhyming texts, pause before saying the rhyming word so students can supply it.
- Involve the students in text innovation where they are able to substitute and manipulate rhymes.

Developing Syllable Awareness

Being able to divide a word into syllables is extremely important for both reading and spelling. The notion of syllables can be quite difficult for some students. When introducing syllables, use only one and two syllable words so the students become comfortable with the concept.

- Use the students' names to clap out syllables.
- Clap the syllables in a name and have the students guess whose name it could be.
- Have students use percussion instruments or clap the syllables when singing or reciting familiar rhymes.
- Have students use physical responses to demonstrate syllables e.g. **snapping fingers, slapping thighs, stomping feet, tapping the desk**.

Developing Onset and Rime Awareness

It is often easier for students to segment words into units larger than individual phonemes. Having students separate words into onset and rime may be one way of making the transition from identifying syllables in words to identifying individual phonemes.

- Use students' names to play with onset and rime. For example, say **"It starts with /r/ and it ends with 'oss ...'**—put it together and it **says ..."** Have the students guess the name.
- Challenge the children to find different onsets to go with the rimes they have produced, e.g. **b – ash, c – ash, cr – ash**.

Common Onsets

All Single Consonants

Initial Consonant Clusters
Two-letter Clusters
/r/ clusters: *br, fr, tr, cr, gr, wr, dr, pr*
/l/ clusters: *bl, cl, fl, gl, pl, sl,*
/s/ clusters: *sc, sk, sm, sn, sp, st, sw,*
others: *tw*
Three-letter Clusters
scr, str, thr, spr, spl, shr, sch, squ

Consonant Digraphs
ch, sh, th, wh

Figure 3.6 Common Onsets

> ## Common Rimes
> ### 37 Most Frequently Used
>
> | | | | | |
> |---|---|---|---|---|
> | ack | ail | ain | ake | ale |
> | ame | an | ank | ap | ash |
> | at | ate | aw | ay | eat |
> | ell | est | ice | ick | ide |
> | ight | ill | in | ine | ing |
> | ink | ip | it | ock | oke |
> | op | ore | ot | uck | ug |
> | ump | unk | | | |
>
> The above can be used to create over 500 English words.
> (Wylie and Durrell 1970)

Figure 3.7 Common Rimes

Developing Phonemic Awareness

Being able to isolate, blend, segment and manipulate phonemes enables readers and writers to manipulate and control words with confidence and ease.

Isolating Individual Phonemes (identifying, matching, oddity and producing tasks)

- Assist students to explore the articulation of phonemes. Encourage them to say each sound and note how their voices and the position of their mouths change with each sound. Give students hand-held mirrors to help them examine the movement of their mouths as the sound is produced.
- Have the students repeat and create tongue twisters. Students' names can be used to create tongue twisters, e.g. **Harry's horses have hairy hooves or Francis found forty famous footballers.**
- Involve the students in picture or word-sorting activities.

Blending and Segmenting (identifying, matching, oddity and producing tasks)

It is important that students have a clear understanding of the concepts represented by the words 'sounds', 'letters' and 'words' before beginning to blend phonemes into words or segment words into phonemes. It is often helpful to combine the teaching of blending and segmenting phonemes with the introduction of print.

- Involve students in activities that require them to count the phonemes in words. Initially choose words with up to three phonemes. Edelen-Smith (1997) suggests that when identifying, blending or segmenting phoneme sequences, a CV pattern e.g. **pie**, should be used before a VC pattern e.g. **egg**, followed by a CVC pattern e.g. **red**.

- Have fun with words by playing with them in speech. For example, have a puppet who overemphasises initial phonemes, saying "P P P-ut the c c c –up on the t t t –able." Encourage the students to 'have-a-go' at talking like the puppet, first together as a whole class and then individually.

- Use an elastic band to illustrate how to stretch words into individual sounds. Say the word at normal speed. Then demonstrate how to say the word slowly, stretching the sounds and stretching the elastic band at the same time.

e.g. *hippopotamus*   *h-i-pp-o-p-o-t-a-m-u-s*

Manipulating Phonemes (Substituting, Deleting, Adding)

- Have students manipulate letters, e.g. **scrabble tiles, magnetic letters or letters made from card** to create or change words.
- Involve the students in playing Sound Take-away.
  - Begin by using compound words from the environment. Select a compound word and demonstrate how to say the word with a part missing. For example. **"This is a football. If I say football without the foot, it says ball. This is a butterfly. If I say butterfly without the fly it says butter."** Have students make up their own from objects in the environment or from pictures provided.
  - Once the students can competently do that with compound words, move on to removing initial or final sounds from words, e.g. **"Pair. It starts with /p/ and ends with air, take the first sound away and it says air."** or **"Card. It starts with car and ends with /d/, take away the /d/ and it says car."** Use the sentence until students are able to delete sounds with a simple prompt such as **"Say 'shout' without the /sh/."** A sound deletion that results in a real word such as 'pair' becoming 'air' or 'treat' becoming 'tree' is easier than one resulting in a nonsense word such as 'book' becoming 'ook' or 'sat' becoming 'sa'.
- Show students how to create new words by adding, deleting or substituting phonemes, e.g. **add /m/ to 'eat' to make 'meat', take the /d/ from 'dear' to get 'ear' or change the /f/ in 'fat' to a /b/ and get 'bat'**.
- Play analogy games: **"I'm thinking of a word. It begins like ball and rhymes with tack. What could it be?"** When the students know more about the alphabet and can do this orally, they can write the words or make them by manipulating letters.

SECTION 2
Teaching Graphophonics

What Is Graphophonics?

Readers co-ordinate many processes and strategies when reading texts. This includes accessing and activating knowledge from the semantic, syntactic and graphophonic cues to make sense of texts. Graphophonic cues help the reader to see the correlation between sounds and symbols in written language.

Graphophonics is defined as the study of sound/symbol relationships as they apply to the alphabetic principle of a written language. The word is derived from:

phonology *n.* study of sounds in a language [f. Gk *phone*—voice, sound]
graph *n.* visual symbol, esp. letter(s), representing a phoneme or other feature of speech [f. Gk *graphe*—writing]

What Students Need to Know

It is important that students understand that letters have a name and represent sounds in words. Letters may represent a number of different sounds depending on their position in the word and the surrounding letters. Letters rarely represent a consistent sound.

For example, the letters 'ea' not only represent the /ē/ sound but they also represent different sounds in the words 'leaf', 'bread', 'steak', 'cereal', 'create' and 'sergeant'. However, some sound/symbol representations are more common than others.

Similarly, students can become confused if led to believe that the letters 'ir' are the only letters that represent the /ûr/ sound. Students will likely come across 'church', 'earth', 'were', and 'work' where different letters are used. By grouping these words together under the /ûr/ sound, teachers are showing students the multiple possibilities of sound/symbol relationships that are inherent in the English language system. The students can then focus on a particular letter pattern. Students will gradually discover the range of sounds and representations as their experience of the written language increases.

ē feet		
e me be	**ea** cream heat meal leaves beaver	**y** thirsty
ee tree bees cheese		**ey** monkey turkey
	ei receive	**eo** people
i ski	**e-e**	**ie** thief chief

Figure 3.8 Multiple Possibilities

For a sound knowledge of graphophonics, students need to be aware of the following understandings.

- Letter names are constant, whereas sounds vary. It is important for students to know the names of the letters of the alphabet to be able to understand which letters represent particular sounds and vice versa.
- Letters can represent different sounds, e.g. **Andrew, Amy, Audrey**.
- Letters sometimes work alone and sometimes in groups, e.g. m**e**, br**ea**d, sh**ee**t t**ea**m.
- The sound that a letter or a group of letters represents depends on where the letter is in a word and what other letters surround it, e.g. **c**at, **c**ity, **C**hristmas, **ch**op.
- The same sound can be represented by different letters, e.g. b**ea**ch, m**e**, k**ey**, sk**i**, th**ie**f.
- The same letter/s may represent different sounds, e.g. r**ough**, c**ough**, d**ough**, pl**ough**.

Researchers, educators and authors all offer different suggestions for the sequence of introducing graphophonic understandings. Most teachers are aware that students do not follow a single, neat order when developing an understanding of symbol/sound relationships. Consider the needs of students and the requirements of any curriculum documents when making decisions about what graphophonic understandings to introduce and when.

The following suggestions have been drawn from a range of resources and provide a number of options.

Routman (1991) suggests:

- Beginning consonants
- Final consonants
- Consonant digraphs (sh, ch, th, wh)
- Medial consonants
- Long vowels
- Short vowels.

The Department of Education, Western Australia (1983) suggests:
When introducing single letters (using letter names and having students discover what different sounds the letters can make) it is advisable to begin with those that are visually very different. One such sequence might be: *s t m b a f c e r o d i h g n y l p u w k v j x z q.*

Badenhop (1992), suggests:
Step 1: teach *p, b; t, d; k, d; s, z; f, v*
Step 2: teach *a, o, i, e, u*
Step 3: teach *m, n, ng, h, w, wh, l, r*
Step 4: teach *th* (the), *th* (moth), *sh, ch, j*
Step 5: teach *ee, ea, ai, ay, oo, oo*
Step 6: teach *c, x, qu, y* (sky, yolk, jelly gym)

Step 7: teach initial and final consonant blends
Initial blends: *sp, st, sc, sk, sm, sn, sl, sw, tw, dw, bl, cl, gl, fl, pl, pr, br, tr, dr, gr, fr*
Final blends: *-st, -ft, -lk, -ld, -pt, -sp, -ct, -lp, -lt, -xt, -nd, -nt, -nch, -mp, -nk*
Three-letter blends: *thr, spr, squ, spl, shr, str, scr*

Step 8: teach long vowel sounds
Long e spellings: *ee, ea, e-e, y*
Long a spellings: *ai, ay, a-e*
Long o spellings: *oe, ow, oa, o-e*
Long u spellings: *ew, ue, u-e*
Long i spellings: *ie, i-e, y*

Step 9: teach remaining diphthongs and r-controlled words
ar, or, ir, er, ur
oi, oy; ou, ow; au, aw

> **Beck, E. (2001) suggests:**
>
> Step 1:
>
> Introduce *a, d, m, s, t, n, **i**, h, **o**, g, p, f, c, b, **e**, sh, k, ck, j, l, **u**, th, r, w, j, x, ch, v, qu, z*; building word lists that use the short vowel sounds e.g. *cat, hit, shop, beg, mug*
>
> Step 2:
>
> Introduce the CVCe pattern e.g. *cake, tube, kite, rode,* where the 'e' is used to create the long vowel sound. The recommended sequence for the CVCe pattern is /a/, /o/, /i/, /u/.
>
> Step 3:
>
> Introduce other common ways of spelling the long vowel sounds e.g. *ea, ee, ai, ay, ow (grow) oi, oy, ou, ow (now)*
>
> Step 4:
>
> Introduce the r-controlled vowels such as *ar, or, er, ir, ur*

> **National Literacy Strategy (1999) suggests:**
>
> Step 1   *s, m, c, t, g, h*
>
> Step 2   *ss, ck, l, n, d, k, sh, ch*
>
> Step 3   *a, e, i, o, u, f, qu, b, r, j, p, th, ng*
>
> Step 4   *v, w, x, y, z*
>
> Step 5   *ai, ee, ie, oa, oo, or, ir, oi, ou*
>
> Step 6   *ay, a-e, ea, igh, y, i-e, o-e, oe, ew, ue, u-e, oy, ow, er, ur, aw, air, ear, oo*

Supporting the Development of Graphophonics

In recent years, there has been some discussion about whether or not graphophonics should be taught in the early years of schooling. It is known that there is a link between students' knowledge of graphophonics and their reading ability, therefore, it is not a question of **whether** graphophonics should be taught, but **how** it can be taught meaningfully.

It is essential that the teaching of graphophonics is explicit and takes place in a context that makes sense to students. When taught as a set of isolated skills, many students often fail to apply their graphophonic knowledge when reading a text. The long-term goal for all students is that they can use graphophonic understandings independently during the reading or writing of texts.

While graphophonic proficiency will assist readers in pronouncing the words on the page, this alone will not guarantee that a reader comprehends the text.

Research suggests that the brain is a pattern detector, rather than an applier of rules (Bransford, Brown and Cocking 1999). If brains are indeed pattern detectors, then it is important to provide students with many opportunities to investigate letter/sound patterns and organise their findings so generalisations can be made. An analytic approach where students 'discover' sounds and rules works best for engaging students in meaningful graphophonic instruction.

Carrying Out Graphophonic Investigations

- After re-reading a text encourage students to find examples of a specific graphophonic understanding in the text.
- Invite students to circle or underline words that contain the focus understanding.
- Once words have been identified, discuss the common features of each word. A sliding mask can be used to isolate any words and to focus attention on its features.

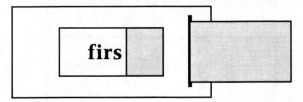

Figure 3.9 Sliding Mask

- List words from the discussion on a chart.
- Ask students to contribute other words, e.g. **words with the /ûr/ sound represented by the letters ir**. If students contribute words that have a different letter representation, e.g. 'church', 'earth', 'worm' accept these words but place them to one side of the chart. It is important at this stage to show students the multiple possibilities that exist. However, it is equally important that students' attention be focused, for explicit teaching, on only one of the multiple possibilities, e.g. 'ir' only.

Ways to spell the /ûr/ sound	
girl	earth
bird	
stir	worm
first	
third	church

Figure 3.10 Ways to Spell the /ûr/ Sound

- Encourage students to search in other texts such as books, charted songs and poems, magazines, modelled writing examples or written messages to find further examples.
- Results of these searches can be recorded in a variety of ways and then used for on-going discussion and investigation.

Pattern	Words that fit	Words that don't fit	Books Reviewed
ea represents /ē/	leaf sea bead	bread great	The Very Hungry Caterpillar Where the Forest Meets the Sea

Figure 3.11a Pattern Chart

We found that the letters sh can go at the beginning, at the end or in the middle of a word.

ship	brush
shut	rush
shed	cash
she	
shine	
	mushroom

Figure 3.11b We Found that the Letters 'sh' 'can'...

How can we spell the /sh/ sound?

sh		ci
ship shut mushroom		special
	s	ti
	sugar	station
	ss	
	tissue	

Figure 3.11c How Can We Spell the /sh/Sound?

The *First Steps Reading Map of Development Second Edition* provides suggestions for appropriate learning experiences for supporting students' graphophonic understandings in each phase of development.

SECTION 3

Vocabulary Knowledge

What Is Vocabulary?

The first vocabulary a child acquires is a listening vocabulary. Most babies are able to respond correctly to spoken words before they are able to produce those words themselves. When students start to read, they begin to acquire a reading vocabulary consisting of words they automatically recognise and understand. They also begin to use words as they compose written texts thus developing a writing vocabulary.

Vocabulary can be described as the list of all the words a person knows. Vocabulary knowledge consists of the following:

- words used when speaking or writing
- words understood when listening
- words that can be decoded and understood when reading
- words automatically recognised and understood when reading (sight vocabulary).

To support the development of reading, it is important to continue to build vocabulary knowledge in each of the above areas.

Sight Vocabulary is the bank of words a reader is able to automatically recognise, pronounce and understand in the context in which it is used. These words are called 'sight words' because effective readers recognise them on sight thus maintaining the speed and fluency required to make sense of an author's message. All readers have a sight vocabulary of words they recognise immediately and effortlessly.

Stating that students recognise these words effortlessly and immediately does not mean that students will learn all words as sight words. However, there are certain words that students can and will recognise by sight as they will encounter these words many times in print. Many of these words have irregular spellings, making them difficult to decode. Without having some words in their sight vocabularies, students' reading will be slow and laborious as they employ word identification strategies to determine the pronunciation and meaning.

What Students Need to Know

When working with students to build their reading vocabulary, Johnson and Pearson (1984) identify three broad categories. Students will benefit from teaching and learning experiences that include vocabulary from all three categories.

- High-Frequency Words
- Selection-Critical Words
- Multi-Meaning Words

• High-Frequency Words

High-frequency words are so called because they occur frequently in all texts. They include function words and concrete words.

Many lists of high-frequency words include function words such as:
- noun determiners, e.g. **the, a, this, that**
- verb markers, e.g. **am, have, may**
- conjunctions, e.g. **and, but, because**
- prepositions, e.g. **by, under, after**
- pronouns, e.g. **he, she, they**.

These words serve particular grammatical functions and are the 'glue' that hold sentences together. Students often have difficulty remembering these words, as they cannot be represented by illustrations, demonstrations or by showing them as objects.

These high-frequency function words occur so often that if students are able to recognise them automatically they can then focus on the meaning of the text. Students need to be able to automatically recognise many of these words as they are difficult to decode using word identification strategies.

Other high-frequency words can be represented by illustrations, demonstrations or objects e.g. **dad, morning, night, school, little, run, red**. These words are relatively easy to learn because they are 'real' to students.

• Selection-Critical Words

Selection-critical words are words that occur frequently in a particular text and a reader must be able to recognise to understand the text. They are specific to a particular topic. For instance, students reading a text about butterflies are likely to encounter words such as **cocoon, caterpillar, antenna, abdomen, thorax, chrysalis** and **life cycle**. Students need to understand these words if they are to successfully understand the overall text. Teachers can help students with these selection-critical words by determining those words that may be problematic. Before reading, students can be involved in activities that will help develop their understandings.

• Multi-Meaning Words

Readers encounter new words regularly but they may not know the meaning of all the words. Once these words are known, they are added to a reader's vocabulary so their vocabulary increases vertically.

A reader will also encounter new words in which they understand the meaning in one context but the same meaning is not transferable to another context. Even the basic lists of high-frequency words contain words that have more than one meaning.

Consider the multiple meanings of the word 'run':
One can:
- run in a race
- run a raffle
- have a run in a stocking or tights
- run a boat aground
- run an errand
- run in an election
- watch the salmon run
- apply paint too thickly causing it to run
- run a car
- run across a friend in the street
- be run out in cricket.

When readers learn new meaning/s for old words, their vocabulary increases horizontally. Both vertical and horizontal development of vocabulary are necessary.

Supporting the Development of Vocabulary

Words are the verbal label that represents a concept or idea. Graves and Graves (1994) make the distinction between vocabulary learning (learning new labels for known concepts) and concept learning. When a concept is totally unfamiliar to the students, they need to develop an understanding of the concept first, and vocabulary can be introduced later. However, if a concept is familiar to the students, then introducing new vocabulary to describe it is a matter of connecting the new words to an already understood concept. For example, if students already understand the concept of **fair** and **unfair**, teaching vocabulary such as **bias, justice, favouritism** or **discrimination** is a matter of introducing new words to the known concept.

first steps

Research supports both the direct teaching and the indirect learning of vocabulary. Certain vocabulary knowledge is acquired indirectly through reading and discussion. (Nagy *et al.* 1985) It also appears that direct teaching is more effective for the acquisition of particular vocabulary. (McKeown and Beck 1988)

Learning Vocabulary Indirectly Teachers can:	Teaching Vocabulary Directly Teachers can:
• Provide Background Experiences	• Teach Specific Words
• Increase Awareness of Words	• Introduce a Range of Word Identification Strategies
• Provide a Wide Range of Everyday Language Experiences	• Teach Students How to Determine the Meaning of Words

Figure 3.12 Ways to Support Vocabulary Development

The *First Steps Reading Map of Development Second Edition* provides further suggestions for appropriate learning experiences for supporting students' vocabulary knowledge in each phase of development.

Learning Vocabulary Indirectly

• *Provide Background Experiences*

Providing students with meaningful first-hand experiences is important for the development and refinement of vocabulary. These experiences can be gained from activities inside or outside the classroom.

If first-hand experiences are not possible, teachers can facilitate the development of vocabulary by providing a range of vicarious experiences through role playing, viewing, speaking and listening or further reading.

• *Increase Awareness of Words*

– Discuss words at every opportunity, pointing out the author's choice and why it is suitable in the context.
– Encourage students to collect and display new and interesting words that they come across in their reading.
– Involve students in meaningful word-play activities.
– Jointly construct Word Walls featuring the words students have collected, e.g. **current topic or theme words, words with unusual spelling patterns, interesting words.**

• *Provide a Wide Range of Everyday Experiences with Language*

Students learn new vocabulary incidentally through everyday experiences with oral and written language.

– Involve students in discussions that require them to explain and defend their ideas.

– Build prior knowledge by giving students the opportunities to discuss topics, themes or issues before reading.

– Provide opportunities for students to interact with a variety of people.

– Provide opportunities for students to read and write for a range of purposes. Reading provides models of rich language that help students learn many new words, and writing provides authentic contexts for students to use those words and develop ownership of them.

– Provide opportunities for students to discuss their reading and the texts they find interesting.

– Provide opportunities for, and encourage students to, read independently.

Teaching Vocabulary Directly

• *Teach Specific Words*

There are two criteria that may be useful when deciding which words should be directly taught to students.

The first group of words are those words that students will see many times in many different contexts. High-frequency words fall into this group.

The second group of words are those that are essential for understanding the major concepts, issues or themes of a text. Words in this group are often called selection-critical words, subject specific words, topic words or technical terms. Where direct teaching of these words is required, teach words in related groups when possible. This will help the student to create relationships among the words so the meaning of the words will develop as the relationships become clearer.

Students working with informational texts or more complex literary texts often have difficulty with the specialised vocabulary they contain.

When beginning a new text or unit of study, ascertain those selection-critical words students already know and those that will need to be introduced.

Once the selection-critical words have been chosen, copy the sentences in which they will appear. Students can then be given an opportunity to say whether or not they know the words presented.

Giving the words a rating such as the following might be useful. (Armbruster, Lehr and Osborn J, 2001).

unknown: the word is totally unfamiliar and the meaning is unknown
acquainted: the word is somewhat familiar and the basic meaning is known
established: the word is very familiar—it is recognised immediately and the meaning in the context in which it is used is known

Students may find it helpful to record and organise the words on a graphic organiser.

How Well Do I Know These Words?		
Unknown Don't know it at all.	**Acquainted** Have seen or heard the word before and I think I know the meaning.	**Established** I know the meaning of the word in this context.

Figure 3.13 How Well Do I Know These Words?

• *Introduce a Range of Word Identification Strategies*

(see this book, Chapter 4, Section 1—Teaching Comprehension and Word Identification Strategies)

• *Teach Students How to Determine the Meaning of Words*

It would be impossible to teach students the meanings of all the words they will encounter. The words that students need to know will vary from student to student as their language backgrounds differ. Instead, consider teaching strategies so students can use them independently to determine the meaning/s of new vocabulary.

The meaning of words can be determined using any of the following.
– Reference Aids
– Morphemic Analysis
– Typographical Aids
– Context Clues.

Reference Aids

References aids include dictionaries, thesauri, 'experts', glossaries or search engines.

Dictionaries provide **all** the meanings of a particular word. Students, therefore, need to consider and choose a meaning that best suits the context in which the word is used.

Glossaries in informational texts are often more useful than dictionaries as they give the definition of a word in the context in which it has been used.

Morphemic Analysis

Morphemes are the smallest units of meaning in words. For example, the word '**unreasonable**' contains three morphemes; '**un**', '**reason**' and '**able**'.

To use morphemic analysis successfully, it is necessary for students to know about the following word parts and the meaning attached to each.
– Prefixes and suffixes
– Base words, including foreign roots
– Compound words.

With constant practice at discovering the meaning of morphemes, students will be able to work out meanings for themselves and make generalisations.

Typographical Aids

Authors include a range of clues that enable readers to determine the meanings of words. These can be typographical aids such as footnotes, italics, bold type, parenthesised definitions, pictures, graphs and charts. Typographical aids can provide a direct reference to an unknown word. Teachers can model how to use these typographical aids so students can work out the meanings of unknown words.

Context Clues

Being able to recognise context clues that enable readers to infer the meaning of new vocabulary is important when reading. Efficient readers tend to recognise context clues automatically. Less efficient readers can be taught how to recognise them. Students should also realise that not all texts provide sufficient context clues for readers to infer the meaning of unknown words.

The following table illustrates some of the ways authors include context clues. Students do not need to be able to define and label these clues; they are provided for teacher reference and as a guide when selecting content to be modelled or discussed with students. Understanding what these clues are and how they work can assist students determine the meaning of unknown words.

Using Context Clues to Infer the Meaning of Unknown Words		
Type of Context	**Clue Definition**	**Example**
Definition	a direct explanation or description is given	A *habitat* is a place where an organism lives.
Linked synonyms	a word is linked with another similar word	Centipedes are very dangerous because they have *venom* or poison which can be released into or onto a victim.
Summary	a word is used to summarise previous concepts	Grazing animals, such as rabbits, kangaroos, elephants and cattle that eat only plant material are called *herbivores*.
Compare or contrast	an antonym or phrase with an opposite meaning is used to define another word	It wasn't a *Conestoga*, like Pa's folks came in. Instead it was just an old farm wagon drawn by one tired horse.
Cause or effect	the cause or result of an unknown word enables the meaning to be inferred	Because the man deliberately tried to get him into trouble, Albert became *irate*.
Example	a word is clarified by the use of an example	All substances can occur in three different *states*. Water, for example, can occur in a solid *state* as ice, in the liquid *state* as water and in a gaseous *state* as steam.
Mood or tone	the meaning of the word can be inferred or hypothesised from the general mood of the sentence.	The *tormented* animal screeched with horror and writhed in pain as it tried desperately to escape from the hunter's trap.

Figure 3.14 Adapted from Vacca R. T. and Vacca J. L. (1989)

The *First Steps Reading Map of Development Second Edition* provides suggestions for appropriate learning experiences for supporting students' vocabulary knowledge in each phase of development.

SECTION 4

Text Form Knowledge

What Is Text Form Knowledge?

Students will encounter an ever-increasing range of texts as they move through school to adulthood. Students will become aware of the purpose, organisation, structure and language features of a range of texts. This knowledge will allow students to determine how to read and understand a text.

What Students Need to Know

It is important for students to develop knowledge of the following features of different forms of text.
• Purpose
• Text Organisation
• Text Structure
• Language Features.

Purpose

Texts are written and read for a reason. Readers can become aware of the decisions that an author makes if they have an understanding of the author's purpose.

Purposes for writing a text include:
– to entertain
– to instruct
– to persuade
– to recount
– to inquire
– to socialise
– to describe
– to explain.

Understanding the purpose for reading can influence the way a text is read. For example, if the purpose is purely for enjoyment, then if the reader momentarily loses concentration, this is unlikely to affect the outcome. However, if the purpose is to learn how to do something, then it is very important that the details and sequences are understood and remembered.

Purposes for reading a text include:
- for enjoyment
- to locate specific information
- to gain a better understanding of the world
- to understand new concepts
- to expand vocabulary
- to make connections to our lives
- to seek answers to problems
- to satisfy curiosity
- to expand imagination
- to learn how to perform a task
- to find good models for writing
- to understand different cultures
- to understand different perspectives and points of view.

Text Organisation

Text organisation refers to the way a text is laid out. The layout also includes the text framework. The term 'text framework' refers to the order in which information is presented. Most texts start with an orientation of some kind. However the content of the orientation will vary according to the text form. For example, the orientation of a recount includes who, when, where and what; while the orientation of a report defines and classifies the subject. Having an understanding of the text framework can help readers to locate specific information.

It is also important for readers to understand the terminology, function and how to use a range of text organisational features, e.g. **headings, sub-headings, diagrams, tables**. The following table summarises many of the organisational features in a text that readers will encounter when reading a range of texts.

Text Organisational Features		
Organisational Feature	**Definition**	**Function**
appendix	extra information included at the end of a text or bound separately	– explains parts of the text by providing more detail
bibliography	a list of information sources cited, used or referred to in the writing of the text	– provides a list of texts for extra reading – acknowledges works quoted – provides evidence so readers can check on authenticity and accuracy

Organisational Feature	Definition	Function
blurb	a short promotional paragraph about the book and/or the author, usually on the back cover	– attracts the reader's interest to the text
bolded or italicised words	words in texts that have been highlighted in some way	– draws the reader's attention to points the author considers to be important
bullet points	a heavy dot used to highlight information	– draws the reader's attention to important points – enables authors to provide information in point or list form
captions	a comment under, above or near an illustration	– explains the content of the diagram, photograph, table or graph – provides an example
computer menu	a pull down or bar list of icons or symbols	– represents commands on the computer – enables the user to select the appropriate command
cross-section	a diagram made by cutting through an object, usually at right angles	– enables the reader to 'see inside' an object
diagram	a visual representation of information presented	– provides more detail – shows a sequence – provides a more simplified view
flowchart	a visual representation of a sequence	– enables readers to follow a process
footnotes	a note, usually in a small font, at the bottom of a page	– supplies extra information about a fact or idea in the main text – cites a reference – directs the reader to other parts of the text
foreword	a short introduction to a text written by someone other than the author	– presents an overview of the text – recommends the text
glossary	a definition of terms used in the text	– explains meaning of words in a particular context
graphs	a pictorial or symbolic representation of data	– enables the reader to make comparison between data – enables the reader to identify trends

first steps

Organisational Feature	Definition	Function
headings	the main title of chapter or large section of a text	– enables readers to quickly find a section or chapter of a text
home page	the opening or main page of a website	– greets visitors – provides information about the website
hyperlink	a segment of text or a graphical item that serves as a cross reference between parts of a hypertext	– enables users to navigate between various sections of a hypertext or from one website to another website
hypertext	a computer based text retrieval system	– enables users to access particular locations within websites by clicking on hyperlinks
index	an alphabetically arranged list of the contents of a text	– provides quick access to specific topics
legend	an explanatory list of symbols used on a map, chart, diagram, table	– provides readers with a quick reference point when trying to identify symbols – assists readers with the interpretation of maps, charts, diagrams, tables
magnifications	enlarged representations of objects, images or models	– enables readers to see a close up of objects, images or models
maps	a representation of a location	– enables readers to find a location – enables readers to compare size, features, position
preface	an introduction to a text written by the author	– provides an explanation of the contents of the text – explains how new edition is different – introduces the text
search engine	a website that searches data bases for specific terms/topics	– gathers and reports requested information from internet websites
side-bar	a short text containing further information, often printed alongside a longer article	– provides additional or contrasting information
site map	a visual or textual model of a website usually organised in hierarchical form	– allows users to navigate the website as they search for specific information

Organisational Feature	Definition	Function
sub-headings	the title of a subsection of a text	– provides a short succinct description of that section of the text – enables the reader to quickly access specific information
symbols	a sign or character used to represent something else	– enables information to be presented briefly – provides a code to interpret diagrams and drawings
table	a framework for recording data	– enables readers to compare data
table of contents	the plan showing the organisation of the text	– provides an overview – enables reader to browse for specific content
timelines	a visual representation of key events	– provides information in a visual form
title page	the page of the text that contains the full title, the author's name, the publisher's name and location	– provides publishing information about a text
website buttons	the symbols or aids used to navigate web-pages	– enables users to quickly move from one part of a website to another, or between related websites

Figure 3.15 Text Organisational Features

Text Structure

The term 'text structure' refers to the way ideas, feelings or information is linked within a text. It is important for students to understand the types of patterns that are used to link and organise information. These include:
– compare and contrast
– cause and effect
– problem and solution
– listing: logical or chronological sequence, collection of details (sometimes called enumeration or description).

These text structures can be found not only in informational texts but also in literary texts. The structure an author chooses to use is often a good indication of the intended message. If readers are aware of the words authors use to signal the text structure, it will assist with comprehension of a text.

Compare and Contrast

A compare and contrast structure attempts to explain how two or more objects, events or arguments are similar and/or different. To understand a compare and contrast text, readers need to link together the comparison and the contrast.

There are many words and syntactic patterns that signal the compare and contrast structure. These include:

similarly	on the other hand
otherwise	but
yet	notwithstanding
the opposing view	not only ... but also ...
in spite of	in contrast
instead	however
meanwhile	although
compared with	different from
alike	

Figure 3.16 Compare and Contrast Words

Other types of words that can be used to indicate the compare and contrast structure include:
– comparatives and superlatives, e.g. **Mount Olympus is <u>high</u>, but Mount Everest is <u>higher</u>.**
– antonyms in subsequent sentences, e.g. **Elephants are <u>herbivores</u>. Lions are <u>carnivores</u>.**
– verbs that imply, compare and contrast, e.g. **Our new house <u>resembled</u> our old house in many ways. The jury <u>deliberated</u> for several hours.**

Cause and Effect

A cause and effect text structure is used to show causal relationships between events. This text structure examines previous circumstances and consequences. To understand a text that uses cause and effect structure, readers are required to:
– recognise the cause and effect relationship
– find the idea associated with the cause and the effect
– use the signal words to link these ideas.

Words used to signal a cause and effect structure include:

because	as a result of
then	so
therefore	accordingly
due to	consequently
nevertheless	this resulted in
if	cause
effect	

Figure 3.17 Cause and Effect Words

The choice of adjectives, nouns and verbs can also imply a cause and effect structure, e.g. **Lack of exercise may lead to obesity. (A causal relationship is implied.)**

Problem and Solution

A problem and solution text structure identifies a problem and then attempts to generate solutions or ways of overcoming the problem. To understand a text that uses problem and solution structure, readers are required to:
– recognise the difficulty
– identify the suggested solutions.

A problem and solution structure and a cause and effect structure are often confused. The difference between the two is that a problem and solution structure implies intervention using a conscious action whereas cause and effect structure does not.

Words used to signal a problem and solution structure include:

one reason for that	a solution to this
the problem is	one response is
this leads to	to prevent
question	answer
trouble	difficulty
solved	propose

Figure 3.18 Problem and Solution Words

Listing (also called Description)

A listing text structure explains the characteristics of people, animals, objects or places. As a broad category, this text structure draws on lists, collections of details and sequences. To understand a text that uses a listing structure, readers need to identify and accumulate the information and order it in some way.

Lists

A list is a set of items related in some way. The way the items are related often provides the title of the list. Lists are usually set out vertically although they can also be embedded in a text, e.g. **When I go to the beach, I take a towel, my hat and some sunscreen.**

A Collection of Details

A collection of details is also a list. Usually these are a series of statements arranged in no particular order.

Sequences

Sequences are also lists. However, the information in these lists has been ordered in some way. The information can be sequenced using time, numerical or spatial order.

Words used to signal a listing structure include:

Collection of Details:	
an example	for instance
such as	and so on
another	in fact
several	
Sequence:	
earlier	finally
after this	next
firstly	secondly
presently	subsequently
in addition	eventually
to begin with	on (date)
below	beside
inside	

Figure 3.19 Listing Words

Language Features

The term 'language features' refers to the type of vocabulary and grammatical structures used in a text. Each text form has specific language features that are appropriate to that form.

These include the following.

– Who or what the text is about. The text participants can be specific, e.g. **Charlotte, My dad** or generalised, e.g. **Bees, Volcanoes.**
– Tense, e.g. **past, present.**
– Use of active voice, e.g. **The oil spill caused the pollution.**
– Use of passive voice, e.g. **The pollution was caused by the oil spill.**

- Type of pronouns. These can be personal, e.g. **my, ours, his, hers** or impersonal, eg. **its.**
- Type of linking words
- Nominalisation—changing verbs to nouns, e.g. **'to compute'** becomes **'the computation'**.
- Word choice, e.g. **precise technical adjectives, action verbs.**
- Style, e.g. **colloquial, formal.**
- Use of direct speech, e.g. **The adviser replied, "It's not our policy to give out that information."**
- Use of indirect speech, e.g. **The adviser said that it was not company policy to report that kind of information.**
- Use of rhyme, rhythm or repetition
- Use of signal words, e.g. **Some words signal different text structures, other words signal choice, linking, conclusions, classification.**

Signal Words for:	
Choice either/or neither/nor another otherwise another possibility alternatively with the exception of whether... or	**Conclusions** in conclusion the findings are findings in summary hence thus on the whole in the main
Linking moreover besides and further in the same way likewise what is more additionally too as well as	**Classification** belongs to is defined as an example of

Figure 3.20 Signal Words

Supporting the Development of Text Form Knowledge

The following table (see Figure 3.21) Overview of Text Form Knowledge, provides a summary of the purpose, organisational framework and language features related to different text forms.

Students can begin developing their text form knowledge by collecting and sorting examples of texts. These examples can then be analysed. Analysing texts involves students focusing on separate sections of texts so they can understand the whole text and how it works. When analysing texts, there is a focus on:
– examining the relationship of the parts to the whole, e.g. **sentences within paragraphs, paragraphs within whole texts**
– collecting, examining and classifying language features
– searching for patterns.

The *First Steps Reading Map of Development Second Edition* provides further suggestions for appropriate learning experiences for supporting students' knowledge of text forms in each phase of development.

Text Forms	Purpose	Organisational Framework *may include some/all of the following*	Language Features and Examples	
narrative, fantasy, adventure, science fiction, fable, fairytale, myth	to entertain	orientation initiating events problem/s resolution	defined characters	*Harry Potter*
			descriptive language	*dark, gloomy*
			dialogue	
			usually in past tense	*was running, thought*
			use of action verbs	*ran, yelled, cried*
			use of personal pronouns	*he, she, they*
			linking words to do with time	*after that, the next morning*
recounts, biography, autobiography, journal, diary, newspaper report	to recount	orientation a series of events in time order re-orientation (optional) evaluation (optional)	specific participants	*My family and I*
			simple past tense	*chased, went, saw*
			action verbs	
			first or third person pronouns	*I, we, hers, his, theirs*
			linking words to do with time	*firstly, secondly, yesterday*
recipe, experiment, instruction manual, rules of a game	to instruct	goal materials method evaluation	generalised and specific participants	*ingredients, batteries the eggs, the rotor*
			reader referred to in a general way, or not mentioned at all	*Player A, each person (You) Draw a semicircle*
			simple present tense	*twist, stir, cut*
			mainly action verbs	*(you) twist, (you) stir*
			detailed factual descriptions	*6 cm, square, red, 400 gm*
			linking words to do with time	*first, then, next*

Text Forms	Purpose	Organisational Framework *may include some/all of the following*	Language Features and Examples	
(cont'd)	(cont'd)	(cont'd)	detailed information on how where when	*carefully, thoroughly* *5 cm from the top* *after replacing the back*
report	to describe	Classification and generalisation description of parts summary	generalised participants	*whales, Australia, satellites*
			action verbs (behaviours)	*climb, erupt, eat, produce*
			timeless present tense	*are, exist, grow*
			factual, precise description	*red and yellow, grey fur*
			technical vocabulary	*marsupials, monotremes*
			third person pronouns	*herself, its, they*
			signal words to compare, contrast, classify	*is similar to but not as belongs to*
explanation	to explain	definition components and parts operation application	generalised participants	*volcanoes, cyclones*
			mainly action verbs	*falls, rises, erupts*
			some passive verbs	*is saturated, was caused*
			timeless present tense	*are, happens, turns, fills*
			signal words to show time cause/effect	*finally, following if/then, so, as a consequence*
exposition, debate, essay, discussion, editorial	to persuade	thesis arguments reiteration	generalised participants, often abstract ideas	*recreational fishermen conservation*
			variety of verb types	
			frequent use of passives	*were caught, is influenced by*
			mainly timeless present tense	
			nominalisation	*computation, calculation*
			signal words – reasoning	*therefore, so, because of*
survey, questionnaire	to inquire	orientation body prompt	generalised participants	*all interviewees*
			mainly action verbs	*use, circle*
			usually in the second person	*Have you?*
			precise language	
			includes question words	*how, when, where, what*
invitation, apology, message, personal correspondence, note	to socialise	orientation body closing	specific participants	*Raoul, Li Chin*
			mainly action verbs	*went, did, enjoyed*
			usually first person	*I, We*
			usually past tense (future for invitations)	*rang, will be held*
			signal words to show time	*in the morning, at 7.00 p.m.*

Figure 3.21 Overview of Text Form Knowledge

CHAPTER 4

Processes and Strategies

Overview

The Processes and Strategies substrand focuses on how students can apply their knowledge and understandings to comprehend and compose texts. Some students employ strategies intuitively, particularly in familiar contexts with familiar people. However, some students will encounter more complex texts and sophisticated purposes in unfamiliar contexts and participants, so students will need to select processes and strategies from a versatile repertoire.

The focus of this chapter is to provide Teaching and Learning Experiences that can be applied to all phases of reading development. Provided are activities that can be easily adapted to meet the needs of students across a range of phases.

This chapter contains the following two sections:
* Section 1—Teaching Comprehension and Word Identification Strategies
* Section 2—Teaching Students to Access and Use Information

Figure 4.1

Teaching Notes: Processes and Strategies for All Phases

These Teaching Notes are designed to be read in conjunction with the Major Teaching Emphases in the Processes and Strategies substrand outlined in the phases of the *First Steps Reading Map of Development Second Edition*.

These notes provide background information for supporting readers to use processes and strategies to identify unknown words, comprehend text and access and use information. The information is organised under the following headings.

- Building Students' Knowledge Within the Cues
- Using Strategies
- Locating, Selecting and Evaluating Texts
- Reflecting on Strategies

Building Students' Knowledge Within the Cues

All readers draw on cues from the three-cueing system to make sense of what they read. This enables readers to relate what is new to what they already know. The three-cueing system consists of **semantic**, **syntactic** and **graphophonic** cues. It is often referred to as the Linguistic Cueing System (Pearson 1976). During the process of comprehending and using text, effective readers use each of these cues interdependently.

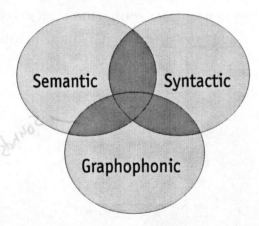

Figure 4.2 Linguistic Cueing System (Pearson 1976)

• *Semantic Cues*

Readers draw on semantic cues to help them know if what they are reading makes sense. Semantic cues are associated with the overall meaning of a text, understanding both the words and the underlying messages. These cues include the reader's cultural and world knowledge, knowledge of the concept, topic, the author or the text type. These cues help readers to make personal associations with a text.

• Syntactic Cues

Readers draw on syntactic cues to help them decide if the text sounds right. Syntactic cues are associated with the structure of the language. These cues include a reader's knowledge of the grammatical features, knowledge of word order in sentences and knowledge of the organisation and structure of whole texts.

• Graphophonic Cues

Readers draw on graphophonic cues to help them identify unknown words. These cues focus on the relationships between sounds and symbols. Graphophonic cues include knowledge of letters, the sounds associated with letters and groups of letters, knowledge of print concepts and knowledge of word structure.

Collectively the knowledge within the three cues makes up an individual's knowledge base. It is critical that students, from a very early age, be provided with opportunities to build their knowledge base within each of the cues. Readers in each phase of development are characterised by growth in this knowledge base.

• Defining the Knowledge Base

All readers have some prior knowledge because of previous experiences. It is the amount of relevant prior knowledge and the activation of that knowledge that determines a reader's success in understanding and assimilating new information. One of the goals of effective teaching is to provide experiences that allow students to build their knowledge base.

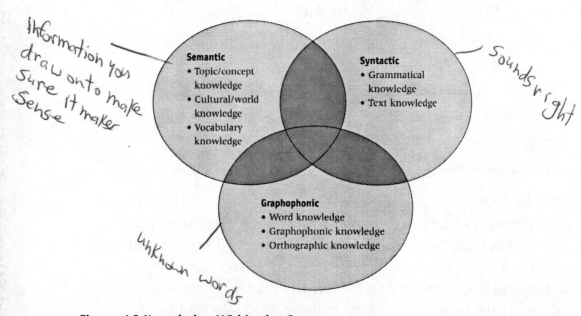

Figure 4.3 Knowledge Within the Cues

• *Topic or Concept Knowledge*

Not all readers have the same amount of prior knowledge on *all* topics or concepts and not *every* reader will have the same amount of knowledge on a specific topic or concepts. The type and frequency of knowledge building experiences provided by the teacher will depend on each student's prior knowledge about a topic or concept.

Teachers can assist students to build their topic knowledge by:
• providing a wide variety of texts
• providing first-hand experiences
• providing vicarious experiences e.g. **demonstrations, multi-media, graphics, speakers or using outside resources**
• talking about the topic from the teacher's own experience
• discussing and analysing texts and experiences.

• *Cultural or World Knowledge*

Cultural or world knowledge consists of a reader's experiences, values, attitudes, beliefs and one's own perceptions of these. Cultural or world knowledge can have a significant impact on the reader's interpretation of a text.

• *Vocabulary Knowledge*

Vocabulary refers to the list of all the words a reader knows. Sight vocabulary refers to the list of words a reader recognises immediately without having to use word identification strategies. Recognition implies that readers can pronounce and understand the meaning of a word in the context in which it is used.

• *Text Knowledge*

Text Knowledge refers to a reader's knowledge of the purpose, structure, organisation and language features of a variety of text forms.
• Purpose refers to the intended outcome as a result of interacting with or composing a text, e.g. **the purpose of a recipe is to instruct, the purpose of debate is to persuade.**
• Text structure refers to the way ideas, feelings and pieces of information are linked in a text, e.g. **compare/contrast, problem/solution, cause/effect, or listing.**
• Text organisation refers to the way a text is organised — the layout, e.g. **paragraphs, diagrams, headings, subheadings, tables.**
• Language features refers to the type of vocabulary and grammar used in a text, e.g. **reports use timeless present tense and precise adjectives.**

• *Grammatical Knowledge*

Grammatical knowledge refers to a reader's knowledge of the patterns of the language. It involves knowing the order in which words are combined to make sentences and paragraphs. Grammatical knowledge includes understandings about the use of punctuation.

• *Graphophonic and Word Knowledge*

Graphophonic knowledge refers to a reader's knowledge of letters and combinations of letters and the sounds associated with them. Word knowledge refers to a reader's knowledge of words, word parts and how words work.

• *Orthographic Knowledge*

Orthographic knowledge refers to the spelling of words in a given language according to established usage. The use of letters is constrained by the position in which they can occur and the allowable sequences. Orthographic knowledge can impact on a reader's word identification and spelling.

Using Strategies

Building the knowledge base within the cues is not enough to ensure that readers will identify unknown words, comprehend texts or access and use information. During the reading process, prior knowledge must be **activated** and **accessed** to help make sense of information in the text. This is achieved by the selection and use of appropriate reading strategies.

Strategies are the mental processes 'you use to do something you want to do'. Reading strategies are used when identifying unknown words, comprehending text and accessing and using information. (See page 114 for a list of strategies.) The explicit teaching of a range of strategies is vital to ensure that students are able to successfully use their prior knowledge to achieve a purpose.

Locating, Selecting and Evaluating Texts

Students at all phases of development locate, select and evaluate texts. It is critical that students are provided with opportunities to build their knowledge base, skills and strategies for locating, selecting and evaluating texts.

• *Locating*

Locating involves knowing what to use to find texts or information in texts for a particular purpose.

• *Selecting*

Selecting involves knowing how to choose the most appropriate text or information in texts to suit a particular purpose. To select texts effectively, students benefit from an understanding of text organisation, an awareness of the available resources, and knowing the most effective strategies to use.

• *Evaluating*

Evaluating involves knowing how to analyse and make judgements about the suitability of a text or information within a text to achieve a particular purpose.

Reflecting on Strategies

Reflecting involves analysing and making judgements about what has been learnt and how learning took place. Students need the opportunity to stop and think about what they have learnt.

Providing time for students to reflect on their reading is important. This helps students to:
• become aware of reading strategies they are using
• monitor the use of their reading strategies
• apply reading strategies in other contexts
• refine their use of reading strategies
• evaluate critically the effectiveness of their use of reading strategies.

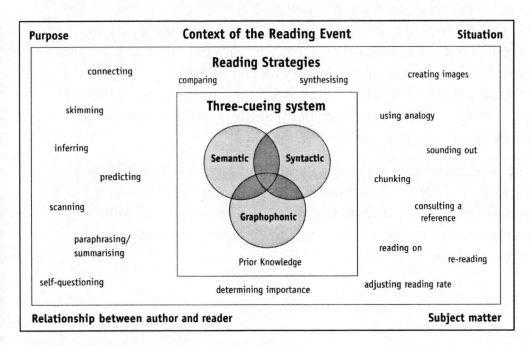

Figure 4.4 Understanding the Reading Process

first steps

SECTION 1

Teaching Comprehension and Word Identification Strategies

Why Teach Strategies?

Effective teachers have an understanding of how reading occurs and are able to plan learning experiences and instruction that support students to become more successful readers. Teachers play an important role in ensuring that all students build up a bank of knowledge that can be accessed during the reading process. Teachers often work tirelessly to ensure that students have knowledge of:

- a growing list of sight words
- graphophonic elements
- grammatical features of the English language
- text structures and organisation
- topics and concepts
- cultural and world matters.

One of the most crucial elements of supporting reading development is the explicit teaching of reading strategies so readers are able to access their prior knowledge during reading. The process of comprehending texts involves much more than the ability to decode words. A reader must actively integrate a range of strategies, including both word identification and comprehension strategies to draw upon all available knowledge in the form of cues. Efficient readers have often automated many of these reading strategies so many occur subconsciously.

The teaching of comprehension and word identification strategies is essential. Explicit demonstrations, on-going scaffolding and opportunities to practise and apply reading strategies will support all readers to identify unknown words, prepare for, monitor and adjust their reading.

What Are the Strategies?

Many teachers have attempted to catalogue a list of the strategies that readers use as they comprehend text. This is a challenging task as the reading process is silent and motionless and involves cognitive strategies that are often not observable.

Reading research over the past two decades has provided insights into the identification of the processes most commonly used by skilled or efficient readers. The work of Keene and Zimmerman (1997) focused on the instruction of strategies used by efficient readers. This work has also provided a springboard for those looking to document specific reading strategies to introduce to students. Although educators will list and categorise strategies in different ways, most lists contain similar elements.

The common element in all work is the focus on what 'good readers' do as they identify words and comprehend text. This focus provides a valid framework for determining the strategies to introduce to students.

Efficient readers are active as they read, simultaneously using a range of processes to identify unknown words and comprehend text. These may include a combination of any of the following processes.
• Clarifying the goal of reading the text (purpose)
• Skimming or looking through a text before reading
• Making predictions about what might be presented next in the text
• Refining predictions as the text is read
• Making connections to what is already known
• Determining which information is the most important in the text
• Re-reading any information considered important or difficult to understand
• Reading on when searching for some specific information
• Making inferences about information not explicitly stated in the text
• Synthesising information in the text to summarise and monitor understanding
• Generating questions about the text
• Creating images from what is read
• Paraphrasing the information read
• Seeking clarification when meaning is lost.

The list of behaviours is not an exhaustive one, but certainly provides useful information about what is important in reading. As a result of the analysis of these behaviours, a list of reading strategies has been compiled. The following strategies are not hierarchical or phase specific. In any reading event a number of reading strategies will be used simultaneously to aid comprehension and/or to identify unknown words.

A List of Reading Strategies

- Predicting
- Connecting
- Comparing
- Inferring
- Synthesising
- Creating Images

- Self-questioning
- Skimming
- Scanning
- Determining Importance
- Summarising and Paraphrasing

- Re-reading
- Reading On
- Adjusting Reading Rate
- Sounding Out
- Chunking
- Using Analogy
- Consulting a Reference

Defining the Strategies

Predicting

Predicting helps readers to activate their prior knowledge about a topic, so they begin to combine what they know with the new material in the text. Predictions are based on clues in the text such as pictures, illustrations, subtitles and plot. Clues for predictions will also come from readers' prior knowledge about the author, text form or content. Students should be able to justify the source of their predictions.

Readers can be encouraged to make personal predictions before and during reading. During reading, effective readers adjust and refine their earlier predictions as new information is gathered and new connections are made. Predictions are usually related to events, actions or outcomes and will be either confirmed or rejected once the text has been read. Students can also use predicting to identify unknown words either before or after decoding. These types of predictions are usually based on the context clues; students need to determine whether the word makes sense in the text.

"From what I know about fishing, I don't think that he will ever be able to catch a shark with that size line and hook."

Figure 4.5

Connecting

Efficient readers comprehend text through making strong connections between their prior knowledge and the new information presented in text. Activating each student's prior knowledge before reading is important. However, students need to be able to continue to use this strategy during reading to continually make connections as they read.

Keene and Zimmerman (1997) categorise the type of connections made by efficient readers.

• **Text-to-Self Connections:** involves readers thinking about their life and connecting their own personal experiences to the information in the text.

• **Text-to-Text Connections:** involves readers thinking about other texts written by the same author or with common themes, style, organisation, structure, characters or content.

• **Text-to-World Connections:** involves readers thinking about what they know about the world outside their personal experience, their family, or their community.

It is important that readers learn to refine and limit their connections to those that help them understand the text better. At first, students may make connections that have little relevance to helping comprehension. By discussing connections, students will be able to focus on how making relevant connections leads to an understanding of texts.

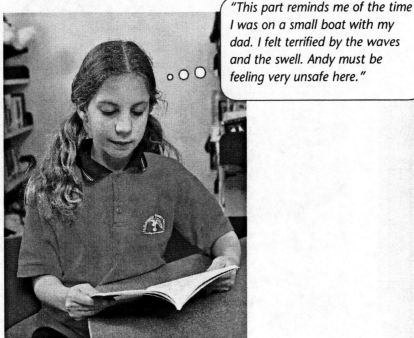

"This part reminds me of the time I was on a small boat with my dad. I felt terrified by the waves and the swell. Andy must be feeling very unsafe here."

Figure 4.6

Comparing

Making comparisons relates closely to the connecting strategy. As students make connections between the text and self, the text and other texts or texts and the outside world, they also begin to make comparisons.

Making comparisons involves students thinking more specifically about the similarities and differences between the connections they are making. When students make comparisons they may begin asking questions, e.g. **How is this different to what I do? How is this text the same as the other one I read? How is this information different to what I believe about this issue?**

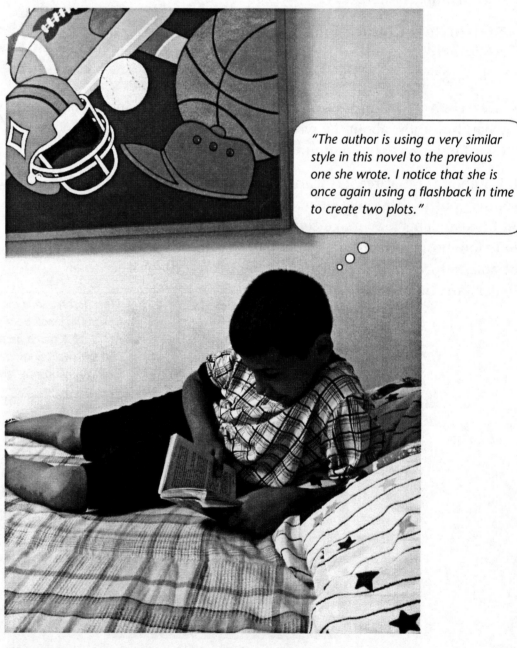

"The author is using a very similar style in this novel to the previous one she wrote. I notice that she is once again using a flashback in time to create two plots."

Figure 4.7

Inferring

Efficient readers take information from a text and add their own ideas to make inferences. During the process of inferring, readers make predictions, draw conclusions and make judgments to create their interpretations of a text. Making inferences allows students to move beyond the literal text and to make assumptions about what is not precisely stated in the text. Inferences made by students may be unresolved by the end of text, neither confirmed nor rejected by the author.

"The lady celebrated when her husband and her son went on the plane to Hawaii. I think she would have been happy to have a spare few days to herself."

Figure 4.8

Efficient readers can also infer the meaning of unknown words using context clues and the pictures or diagrams.

Synthesising

When comprehending text, efficient readers use synthesising to bring together information that may come from a variety of sources. Synthesising involves readers piecing information together, like putting together a jigsaw. As students read and use synthesising, they stop at selected places in a text and think about what has been read. This encourages them to keep track of what is happening in the text.

Students who are consciously aware of using this strategy are able to continually monitor their understanding of text. During the process of synthesising, students may be connecting, comparing, determining importance, posing questions and creating images.

"So, this bit helps me understand why Grandpa left the farm. He just couldn't do all the jobs alone."

Figure 4.9

Creating Images

Efficient readers use all their senses to continually create images as they read text. The images that individuals create are based on their prior knowledge. Sensory images created by readers help them to draw conclusions, make predictions, interpret information, remember details and assist with overall comprehension. Images may be visual, auditory, olfactory, kinesthetic or emotional.

Students may need extra encouragement to create images with lots of detail or those that go beyond the literal information in the text. Support can also be provided to help students revise their images when new information is gained.

It is important that students are also given the opportunity to share their images and to talk about how creating images helps them gain a better understanding of the text. Images can be shared orally, as drawings, as jottings or through drama.

"I think the house is really old and dilapidated, with creepers all over it".

Figure 4.10

Self-questioning

Efficient readers continually think of questions before, during and after reading to assist them to comprehend text. Often these questions are formed spontaneously and naturally, with one question leading to the next. Questions may relate to the content, style, structure, important messages, events, actions, inferences, predictions, author's purpose, or may be an attempt to clarify meaning. Self-formulated questions provide a framework for active reading, engaging students in the text as they go in search of answers. Students need to be aware that answers to all questions may not always be in the text.

Helping students to become aware of questions they naturally ask is an important goal for teaching this strategy. Encouraging students to understand how the generation of questions helps to develop a deeper understanding of the text being read is also important.

"I wonder where the dad is in this story? Did she ever know her dad at all?"

Figure 4.11

Skimming

Skimming involves glancing quickly through material to gain a general impression or overview of the content. This involves the reader passing over much of the detail to get the general gist of what the text contains. Skimming is often used before reading to:

• quickly assess whether a text is going to meet a purpose
• determine what is to be read
• determine what's important and what may not be relevant
• review text organisation
• activate prior knowledge.

Students can be helped to use skimming by being encouraged to check any graphics, and read all underlined, italicised or highlighted text as well as titles and subheadings.

"I think this pamphlet is going to be useful for my project. I can see by the headings and pictures that it includes information about habitat, breeding, food, hunting and behaviour of lions. This should be great."

Figure 4.12

Scanning

Scanning involves glancing through material to locate specific details such as names, dates, places or some particular content. For example, a reader might scan a contents page or index to find the page number of a specific topic; a reader may scan a dictionary or telephone book in search of a particular word or name or a reader may scan as they re-read a text to substantiate a particular response.

"From the list of options generated by my search, this website looks the best. It states that it contains photographs of lions, which is what I'm looking for."

Figure 4.13

Beginning readers may also scan a text looking for picture clues that may help them identify any unknown words.

Determining Importance

Efficient readers constantly ask themselves what is most important in this phrase, sentence, paragraph, chapter, or whole text. Students benefit from understanding how to determine the important information, particularly in informational and website texts. Factors such as purpose for reading, knowledge of topic, prior experiences, beliefs and understanding of text organisation will help readers to identify important information in a text.

Students can begin to identify important concepts or ideas from short pieces of texts. Key words, phrases and sentences can then be identified. It is beneficial to begin with informational texts and highlight organisational features that will help students to decipher important information from less important information. These features include; headings, subheadings, titles, illustrations, bolded text, icons, hyperlinks and font size. Students also need opportunities to determine important information in literary texts.

"Oh this is the part about food and hunting. I will underline the key words. I think *varied diet,* and *female's duty are important.*"

Figure 4.14

Summarising and Paraphrasing

Linked closely to the strategy of determining importance, summarising and paraphrasing are part of the process of identifying, recording and writing the key ideas, main points or most important information from a text into your own words.

Summarising is the ability to reduce a larger piece of text so the focus is on the most important elements in the text. The re-stating or re-writing of text into other words is referred to as paraphrasing. Summarising and paraphrasing involve using the key words and phrases to capture the main focus of text.

"I think the purpose of this piece of text was to help me understand that explorers knew much less about the world than we do today."

Figure 4.15

Re-reading

Efficient readers understand the benefits of re-reading whole texts or parts of texts to clarify or enhance meaning. Reading or hearing a text more than once can be beneficial for all readers, allowing them to gain a deeper understanding of the text.

Re-reading can also be used as a word identification strategy. Efficient readers sometimes re-read to work out the meaning of difficult words using context clues. The opportunity to re-read a text also helps to improve fluency.

Reading On

When students cannot decode an unfamiliar word in a text, they can make use of the reading on strategy. Skipping the unfamiliar word and reading on to the end of the sentence or the next two or three sentences often provides the reader with sufficient context clues to help determine the unknown word. Once the unknown word has been determined, students can re-read that section of the text. Reading on can also be used with larger chunks of text in an attempt to clarify meaning that may have been lost. For example, reading on to the end of a section, page or chapter can often support understanding.

"I'm not sure what this word is, I'll skip it, keep reading to the end of the sentence and see if that gives me a clue."

Figure 4.16

Adjusting Reading Rate

It is important that students allow themselves to adjust their reading rate or pace and recognise when this may be necessary. The purpose for reading often determines the most appropriate rate. Readers may slow down to understand new information, clarify meaning, create sensory images or ask questions. Readers may speed up when scanning for key words or skimming to gain an overall impression of a text.

"I'll quickly read the headings and pictures of this web page to see if it will give me some information about the habitat of reptiles."

Figure 4.17

Sounding Out

Readers use their knowledge of letter-sound relationships to take words apart, attach sounds to the parts and blend the parts back together to identify unknown words. Sounding out phonemes is often used as a strategy to decode unknown words.

Chunking

As readers encounter greater numbers of multi-syllabic words, they can be encouraged to break words into units larger than individual phonemes. Readers might chunk words by pronouncing word parts such as onset and rime, letter combinations, syllables or parts of the word that carry meaning.

Using Analogy

Readers use analogy when they refer to words they are familiar with to identify unknown words. They transfer what they know about familiar words to help them identify unfamiliar words. When using analogy, students will transfer their knowledge of common letter sequences, onset and rimes, letter clusters, base words and word parts that carry meaning or whole words.

Consulting a Reference

The use of word identification strategies such as 'sounding out' or 'chunking' may unlock both the pronunciation and meaning of words. However, if the word is not in a reader's vocabulary, the reader will not be able to understand the meaning to the word. Consulting a reference is an additional strategy that enables students to unlock the meaning of a word. Being taught how to use a dictionary, thesaurus, reference chart or glossary will help students locate the meanings, pronunciations or derivations of unfamiliar words.

How to Teach the Strategies

The remainder of this section will focus specifically on the explicit teaching of strategies associated with identifying unknown words and comprehending texts. Before reading strategies can be taught, it is critical for teachers to have an understanding of what efficient readers do and the strategies they use while reading. The long-term goal for all students is that they can select and use strategies flexibly and independently during any reading event.

The use of a reading strategy rarely happens in isolation; it often involves simultaneously using a number of strategies such as connecting, predicting and inferring. Students should be introduced to a variety of strategies and understand how these strategies work together.

It is also appropriate to focus on an individual reading strategy where it is introduced and practised over a period of time. A unit of work focusing on one strategy may consist of a combination of demonstrations, think-alouds, time for practice and opportunities to apply the strategy across other curriculum areas. It is also important to help students understand how different strategies can work together. A variety of authentic texts, including literary and informational, can be selected to support the instruction of a particular strategy.

Figure 4.18 is based on *The Gradual Release of Responsibility* model (Pearson and Gallagher 1983). The use of this framework will help teachers plan for the effective introduction of reading strategies. The framework involves moving students from a supportive context where the teacher has a high degree of control (modelling) to a more independent context where the student has more control (independent application).

There are four effective teaching practices outlined in this framework: modelling, sharing, guiding and applying. By using a balance of these practices sequentially and recursively, and providing a variety of opportunities, teachers can help students use a range of reading strategies.

Teachers can provide opportunities for students to:
• actively attend to a variety of 'strategy' demonstrations
• hear the thinking behind the use of each strategy
• contribute ideas about the use of strategies in supportive whole-group situations
• work with others to practise the strategies
• receive feedback and support the use of strategies from the teacher and peers
• independently read and practise the strategies with a range of texts
• apply the strategies in authentic reading situations across the curriculum.

	Modelling	Sharing	Guiding	Applying
Role of the Teacher	The teacher demonstrates and explains the reading strategy being introduced. This is achieved by thinking aloud the mental processes used when using the strategy.	The teacher continues to demonstrate the use of a strategy with a range of texts inviting students to contribute ideas and information.	The teacher provides scaffolds for students to use the strategy. Teacher provides feedback.	The teacher offers support and encouragement as necessary.
Role of the Students	The students participate by actively attending to the demonstrations.	Students contribute ideas and begin to practise the use of the strategy in whole-class situations.	Students work with help from the teacher and peers to practise the use of the strategy using a variety of texts.	Students work independently to apply the strategy in contexts across the curriculum.

Degree of Control

Figure 4.18 Teaching Reading Strategies Using a Gradual Release of Responsibility Approach

Modelling

Modelling is the most significant step when teaching any reading strategy. Conducting regular, short sessions that involve modelling and thinking aloud will show how an effective reader makes use of a particular strategy.

By using the practice of modelling to introduce new reading strategies, teachers are able to articulate what they are thinking as they read silently. The reading process will become obvious to students. Thinking aloud is a vital part of the modelling process. When introducing a new strategy, consider planning for multiple demonstrations of how to use the strategy and its benefits.

Modelling sessions need to be well planned and thought out. It is more effective to think through what needs to be modelled and where in the text that might happen, than to make spontaneous comments as the text is being read.

Planning Modelling Sessions

Consider the following questions, prior to modelling for students, so modelling sessions are effective and successful.

1 How do I use this strategy in my own reading?
2 How does this strategy help me become a more efficient reader?
3 What is important for students to know about this strategy?
4 Which texts might be the most appropriate to model this strategy?
5 Where in this text will it be possible to demonstrate the use of the strategy?
6 What language can I use to best describe what I am doing and my thinking?

A Strategy Demonstration Plan (see Figure 4.19) may also help to create a successful modelling session. Demonstration Plans are completed prior to sessions and help to keep sessions focused.

Conducting Sessions to Model the Use of Strategies

• Introduce the name of the strategy. Explain what it means.
• Explain why it is useful and how efficient readers use it.
• Explain to students that modelling involves times when the text is being read and times when thinking is being described. Alert students to how they will know what is happening, e.g. **laying down book or looking up**.
• Begin reading text to students, stopping at selected places to think aloud. Use precise, accurate language to describe the thinking while demonstrating the use of the selected strategy.

- Invite students to discuss their observations of the demonstration, e.g. "What did you notice? What language did you hear me use?"
- If appropriate, jointly construct a chart listing the key points about the use of the strategy or the type of language that can be used.

Strategy Demonstration Plan	
Strategy to Be Introduced:	
When and Why It Is Useful:	
Key Points to Model: • • • •	
Text Selected:	
Pages to Be Used:	Language to Describe My Thinking

Figure 4.19 Strategy Demonstration Plan for Teacher Use

When we Predict
Look at the
. text title
. front and back covers
. dust jacket
. blurb
. pictures
. table of contents

Think about the
. topic
. author
. text form

Making Connections
Questions to Ask

What do I already know about this topic?

What do I already know about this author?

What do I already know about this text form?

Does this remind me of anything?

Figure 4.20a: When We Predict

Figure 4.20b: Making Connections—Questions to Ask

Sharing

Sharing sessions provide the opportunity for students and teacher to think through texts together. In these sessions, the teacher continues to demonstrate the use of the selected strategy. However, the major difference between modelling and sharing sessions is that students are now invited to contribute ideas and information during these demonstrations.

Thinking aloud during sharing sessions is an opportunity for the teacher to demonstrate the use of a selected strategy and enables individual students to participate. For example, while the text is being read and a strategy being demonstrated, students can be asked to share how they are using the strategy, e.g. **"What connections are you making?"** Inviting different students to share their thinking will allow others to hear a range of ideas which is important when teaching reading strategies.

It is beneficial to use a variety of informational and literary texts for demonstrations during sharing sessions. As students begin sharing their use of the strategy, the jointly constructed strategy charts can be refined. Created over time, these cumulative charts document how to make use of a particular strategy.

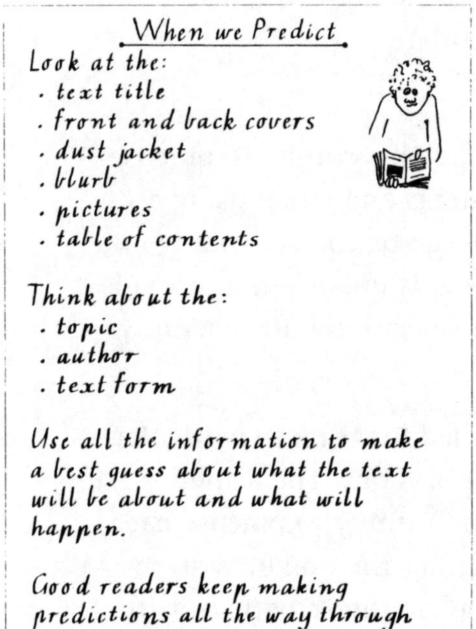

When we Predict

Look at the:
. text title
. front and back covers
. dust jacket
. blurb
. pictures
. table of contents

Think about the:
. topic
. author
. text form

Use all the information to make a best guess about what the text will be about and what will happen.

Good readers keep making predictions all the way through the text.

Figure 4.21a When We Predict

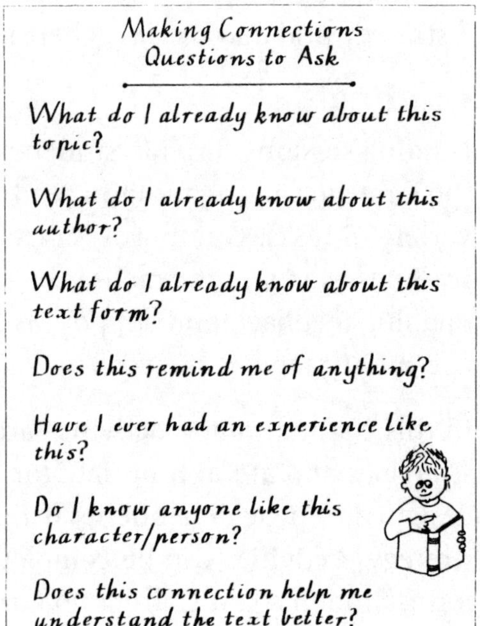

Making Connections
Questions to Ask

What do I already know about this topic?

What do I already know about this author?

What do I already know about this text form?

Does this remind me of anything?

Have I ever had an experience like this?

Do I know anyone like this character/person?

Does this connection help me understand the text better?

Figure 4.21b What Can I Do When I Don't Know a Word

Planning Sharing Sessions

Considering the following questions, prior to sharing sessions with students, will help to maintain the focus of sharing sessions.

1 What aspects of the strategy do I need to further demonstrate?
2 Which texts might be the most appropriate to reinforce this aspect of the strategy?
3 What language associated with this strategy do I want to review?
4 How can I best involve the students in contributing to the demonstrations?
5 Will I create an opportunity to add to a class cumulative strategy chart?

Conducting Sharing Sessions to Continue the Demonstration of Strategies

- Re-introduce the strategy. Invite students to explain what it means.
- Elicit from the students why it is useful and how effective readers use it.
- Begin reading text to students, stopping at selected places to think aloud and demonstrate the use of the strategy. Use precise, accurate language to describe the thinking involved.
- Invite students to make use of the strategy throughout the demonstration and share their thinking.
- Provide constructive feedback and positive comments about students' use of the strategy.
- Summarise different ways that individuals made use of the strategy and add to class chart if appropriate.

Guiding

Guiding sessions provide students with the opportunity to practise the strategies in meaningful reading contexts and when using a variety of texts. Guiding sessions involve the teacher providing scaffolds as students practise the strategy. It is important to provide ongoing feedback and support as students begin to independently use the strategy.

In this chapter, many activities are provided that link to particular strategies and are appropriate for guiding sessions. The activities are designed to provide students with the opportunity to practise each strategy. Activities can be completed in either the oral or written form. Students can share a text and complete the activity in pairs or small groups.

Planning Guiding Sessions

Consider the following questions, prior to students completing any practice activity, so guiding sessions are effective and successful.

1 Which strategy do my students need to practise?
2 Have I provided multiple demonstrations about the use of the strategy?
3 Have I provided many opportunities for sharing sessions where we have discussed and used the strategy?
4 What texts do I want the students to use to practise the strategy?
5 Which activity might I use to provide a scaffold for the practice session?
6 What is the most effective way for the students to record their work?
7 What grouping arrangements will be most suitable for the students?
8 How will I provide feedback to the students during the activity?
9 How will I provide the opportunity for students to reflect on and share their learning after completing the activity?

Conducting Guiding Sessions to Practise the Use of Strategies

• Select texts to be used for both demonstration and independent student use.
• Re-introduce and discuss the strategy.
• Model the use of the strategy, using a specific practice activity.
• Provide time for students to work with partners or in small groups to read an allocated text.
• Provide time for students to complete the activity.
• Provide constructive feedback and support where necessary.
• Encourage students to share completed activities.
• Encourage students to reflect on the use of the strategy.

Applying

Students will benefit from opportunities to work independently and apply the use of strategies learnt in all reading situations. It is important to encourage students to make use of reading strategies when working in other curriculum areas.

Teachers can continue to talk about and demonstrate the application of any strategies when sharing texts from across the curriculum. Ongoing modelling of how and when strategies can be applied and how they assist readers to identify unknown words and comprehend text will encourage students to use strategies beyond planned classroom reading activities.

Guided Practice Activities

The following activities are just some of those available that provide students with support and scaffolding as they practise each reading strategy.

Before selecting an activity, consider the student needs, the type of text being used, the grouping of the students and the desired outcomes. When selecting an activity it is also worthwhile to note the following:

- Activities are not related to age, grade or phase.
- Activities for each strategy are listed in order from the simplest to the more complex.
- Activities can be used with a wide range of texts. Some activities may be more suitable to use with informational text while other activities may be more suitable to use with literary text. Some activities could be suitable or be adapted to use with both types of text.
- Students may feel more supported by doing the activities with a partner or in small groups.
- Many of the activities could be used to practise a range of reading strategies, not only for the suggested strategy.

Guided Practice Activities for Reading Strategies

Reading Strategies / Practice Activities	Predicting	Connecting	Comparing	Inferring	Synthesising	Creating Images	Self-questioning	Skimming	Scanning	Determining Importance	Summarising/Paraphrasing	Re-reading	Reading On	Adjusting Reading Rate	Sounding Out	Chunking	Using Analogy	Consulting a Reference
Split Images (page 133)																		
Personal Predictions (page 133)																		
Check the Text (page 134)																		
Crystal Ball (page 134)																		
Think Sheet (page 134)																		
Extended Anticipation Guides (page 135)																		
Connecting with the Text (page 137)																		
Before-and-After Chart (page 138)																		
Think and Share (page 138)																		
Linking Lines (page 139)																		
What's in a Text? (page 140)																		
Venn Diagrams (page 141)																		
Like or Unlike? (page 141)																		
Just Like (page 142)																		
Double Entry Journal (page 142)																		
Character Self-Portrait (page 144)																		
Interviews (page 145)																		
Rating Scales (page 145)																		
Report Card (page 147)																		
What's My Point of View (page 147)																		
Developing Dialogue (page 148)																		
Turn on the Lights (page 148)																		
Plot Profile (page 149)																		
Great Debate (page 150)																		
Synthesis Journal (page 150)																		
Picture This! (page 151)																		
Sensory Chart (page 152)																		
Post Your Senses (page 152)																		
Changing Images (page 153)																		
Open Mind Portrait (page 153)																		
Information Images (page 154)																		
Clouds of Wonder (page 155)																		

Practice Activities / Reading Strategies	Predicting	Connecting	Comparing	Inferring	Synthesising	Creating Images	Self-questioning	Skimming	Scanning	Determining Importance	Summarising/Paraphrasing	Re-reading	Reading On	Adjusting Reading Rate	Sounding Out	Chunking	Using Analogy	Consulting a Reference
Stop-and-Think Cards (page 156)																		
BDA Questions (page 156)																		
Written Conversation (page 157)																		
Picture Flick (page 158)																		
Graphic Overlays (page 158)																		
Sneak Preview (page 159)																		
Hunt the Text Challenge (page 160)																		
Beat the Buzzer Quiz (page 161)																		
Retrieval Charts (page 161)																		
Interesting Words Chart (page 162)																		
What's Your Story? (page 163)																		
Famous-Five Key Word Search (page 164)																		
Very Important Points (page 165)																		
Main Idea Pyramid (page 165)																		
Oral Summaries (page 166)																		
Reciprocal Retells (page 166)																		
Main Idea Sort (page 167)																		
Newspaper Report (page 167)																		
66 Words (page 168)																		

Figure 4.22 Guided Practice Activities for Reading Strategies

READING STRATEGY: PREDICTING

Guided Practice Activities

1 Split Images
2 Personal Predictions
3 Check the Text
4 Crystal Ball
5 Think Sheet
6 Extended Anticipation Guides

Simple to complex

1 Split Images

Participating in a Split Images activity involves students taking turns to view and describe illustrations in a text to a partner. Texts should be short, unfamiliar and have a strong, progressive plot. Illustrations need to be clear and provide sufficient information to enable students to make informed predictions.

• Form students into pairs.
• Direct students to take turns to view a page with an illustration and describe it for his or her partner. (The other half of the pair is not permitted to look.) For example, **"There are two cats. One of them has a bandage on its paw and the other one is asleep in a basket …"**
• Explain to students that they can include predictions about the illustrations, e.g. **"I think the cat with the sore paw is sad because …"**
• Direct the other student to view the next illustration and to describe it while building onto their partner's prediction or storyline. This process of alternating between students to describe the illustrations continues until the text is completed.
• Ask partners to share their interpretation of the whole text. Re-examine the pictures if needed.
• Read or provide time for students to read the text. Encourage students to compare the text to the information that was conveyed in the illustrations.

2 Personal Predictions

Completing a Personal Predictions activity format provides students with the opportunity to build some expectations of a text, activate their background knowledge and to preview material before reading.

• Invite students to look and read the title, author and cover page to make and record an initial prediction about the text. This can be done individually.

- Provide a selection of key words from the text. Ask students to sort the key words into categories such as characters, setting and events.
- Direct students to individually use the sorted words to record a second prediction.
- Provide time for students to share predictions with a partner or in a small group, to compare and substantiate thoughts and ideas with others.
- Provide time for students to read the text.
- Encourage students to reflect on similarities and differences between predictions made and the actual text.

3 Check the Text

Check the Text is an activity that works successfully when completed as a small group or partner activity. Completing a Check the Text activity helps students to use pictures, photographs, diagrams or illustrations to make predictions about the text. Teachers cover the text so that students can only see the diagram, pictures or photographs.

- Provide time for students to examine and discuss any diagrams, illustrations or photographs in a text.
- Direct students to create text that matches the diagrams, illustrations or photographs.
- Invite students to compare their version with the actual text.

4 Crystal Ball

The Crystal Ball activity encourages readers to draw on explicit and implicit information from a text. Once the whole text has been read, students speculate about the future of a main character.

- After reading a text, form students into small groups. Each group is allocated a character from the text.
- Have students brainstorm important information about their character's likes, dislikes, interests or personality that were stated explicitly or implied in the text.
- Invite students to create a future for the character, e.g. **where they are, what they are doing, who they are with**. Predictions should stem from the information in the text.
- Encourage students to share Crystal Ball predictions and substantiate speculations.

5 Think Sheet

Think Sheets (Raphael 1982) consist of a series of chapter titles, headings or subheadings taken directly from the text that will be read to students. They can use the questions to make and record predictions about what information may be in the text.

Students can complete Think Sheets independently, although the discussion about predictions and substantiations is extremely valuable.

- Prepare a Think Sheet by rewriting some headings or subheadings from the chosen text into questions.
- Before reading the text, direct students to work with a partner to consider, discuss and record what the answers might be to the questions.
- Have students record their predictions in the *Before Reading Prediction* section of the chart.
- Provide time for students to read the text and record the relevant information for each question. This is recorded in the *What the Text Says* section of the format.
- Have students compare their predictions with the text.

Adaptations:

Predictions may be drawn or simply entered as key words. Once students are familiar with the use of Think Sheets, they could create their own questions from the headings and subheadings of the text.

6 Extended Anticipation Guides

An Anticipation Guide consists of a series of statements about a particular topic. The statements may reflect common misconceptions or consist of accurate information. Prior to reading, students use their existing knowledge to categorise statements as either true or false. Students then read the text to confirm or reject their predictions. The Extended Anticipation Guide (Duffelmeyer, Baum and Merkley 1987) encourages students to substantiate their findings by referring to the text and using their own words to explain concepts.

Think Sheet

Question:
What is the ozone layer?

Prediction (Before Reading):
A layer of gas that protects the Earth

What the Text Says (After Reading):
Ozone is an unstable gas, continuously made and destroyed in the Earth's atmosphere. The ozone layer prevents the Sun's invisible but harmful rays from reaching the Earth.

Question:
What has caused the ozone hole?

Prediction (Before Reading):
Overuse of aerosol cans

What the Text Says (After Reading):
Mainly due to man-made chemicals that contain chlorine or bromine. Also the huge quantities of ash and dust in the atmosphere following a volcanic eruption.

Question:
How does the ozone hole affect us on Earth?

Prediction (Before Reading):
Suns rays cause sunburn and cancer.

What the Text Says (After Reading):
More UV rays reach the Earth - these can cause blindness, sunburn, cancer, affect the ability of the body to fight off some infectious diseases, slows down plant growth

Figure 4.23 Student Sample Think Sheet

Students can complete Extended Anticipation Guides independently, although the discussion about predictions and location of specific details that confirm or reject early predictions is extremely valuable.

• Write statements from a text that are either true or false. List statements in the order that the information appears in the text. Focus on the key ideas in the text, including those that are implicit. The statements should be short and include frequent misconceptions about the topic.

• Prior to reading the text, ask students to mark the statements predicting whether the statements are true or false.

• Provide time for students to discuss their predictions and substantiate their point of view by drawing upon their prior knowledge.

• Have students read the text to confirm or reject their predictions. Students record if the statements are true or false based on the information in the text. Students can supply references to show where the information was found, e.g. **paragraph two, page four**.

• Provide time for students to discuss and compare the information in the text with their predictions.

Extended Anticipation Guide			
Text 'Animals of the World'		Author S. Roberts	
SELECTED STATEMENTS FROM THE TEXT	Before Reading I think this statement is true/false	After Reading This statement was true/false	Reference
Animals use other ways to smell if they don't have a nose.	False	True	Page : 2 Para : 3
Some animals grow a new body part after a part has been lost.	True	True	Page : 3 Para : 1
Animals reproduce either by laying eggs or giving live birth.	True		
Not all animals need sunlight to exist.			

Figure 4.24 Student Sample Extended Anticipation Guide

READING STRATEGY: CONNECTING

Guided Practice Activities

1 **Connecting with the Text**

2 **Before-and-After Chart**

3 **Think and Share**

4 **Linking Lines**

5 **What's in a Text?**

1 Connecting with the Text

Using a Connecting with the Text framework helps students to make personal connections with a text while reading.

• Provide students with stick-on notes to use while reading a text. Students use these to signal any connections they make while reading a text. These connections may be related to personal experiences, other texts they have read, similar characters, things they have done, or something else they know about.

• Provide time for students to complete the Connecting with the Text chart using the jottings they made while reading.

• Encourage students to share their responses with other students and make comparisons between the connections made.

Connecting with the Text

This story reminds me of a time when *My grandad would take us on unusual, fun outings. He always let us do the things Mum wouldn't let us do.*

This story reminds me of the text *I'll Love You Forever* because *it's also about a child and mother relationship. In I'll Love You Forever the child character is a male.*

The character *of the daughter* reminds me of *Miss Nancy in W.G.M. Partridge* because *she also liked to remember things about her childhood.*

I think knowing something about *being a daughter.*

helped to understand this text

Figure 4.25 Student Sample Connecting with the Text

2 Before-and-After Chart

The Before-and-After Chart is a way of organising information elicited through brainstorming sessions and supporting students to make connections to what they know about a topic before reading. Adapted from Ogle (1986), the *Before* section of this chart provides space to record what is known before reading. The *After* sections provide a real purpose for reflecting on reading to find out what has been learnt and what is yet to be learnt.

- Allow time before reading for students to brainstorm any information they know about the selected topic. This information is recorded in the form of key words or phrases and placed onto the *Before* column titled *What I/We Know About* _____.
- After reading, provide time to record all the new information learnt. This is recorded in the *After* column titled *What I/We Have Learnt*. Have students read back over their brainstormed information and check if it was referred to in the text they read.
- Encourage students to consider any information they would still like to find out. This can be entered in the space titled *What I/We Still Want to Find Out* and can provide motivation for further reading or research.

Adaptations:

A Before-and-After Chart could be completed over time. The initial brainstorm of what we know and what we have learnt may take two sessions.

Once the students are familiar with the structure of a Before-and-After Chart and the process of using it, add another column. The title of this column could be 'Best Search Words'. Discuss and record in this column the best words to use when locating further information from search engines, indexes and contents pages.

3 Think and Share

Completing a Think and Share activity provides an opportunity for students to make comparisons between characters within a story, as well as make connections to their own experiences.

- Provide time for students to work in small groups to list the key events of a shared text. Have each student in the group list the events. (See the following chart as an example.)
- Allocate a character to each student or pair of students in the small group.
- Direct students to reflect on each event and consider what their character was feeling and thinking during each event. These feelings and thoughts can be recorded in the second column.

- Encourage students to take on the role of their character as they share and compare reactions, feelings, thoughts and justifications of actions.

Adaptations:

The whole class can easily complete this activity. Allocate a particular character to small groups. Each small group then considers certain events from their character's perspective. A jigsaw process can then be used to share and compare information across groups.

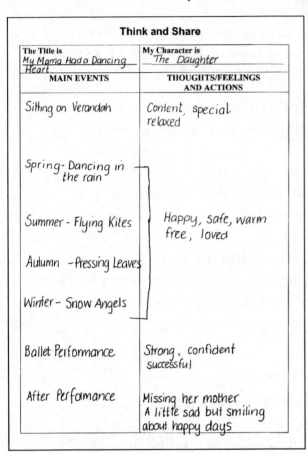

Think and Share

The Title is My Mama Had a Dancing Heart	My Character is The Daughter
MAIN EVENTS	**THOUGHTS/FEELINGS AND ACTIONS**
Sitting on Verandah	Content, special relaxed
Spring- Dancing in the rain	Happy, safe, warm free, loved
Summer - Flying Kites	
Autumn -Pressing Leaves	
Winter - Snow Angels	
Ballet Performance	Strong, confident successful
After Perfomance	Missing her mother A little sad but smiling about happy days

Figure 4.26 Student Sample Think and Share

4 Linking Lines

Completing the Linking Lines activity helps readers make connections between texts.

After re-reading favourite texts, students draw lines between text titles, explaining how the texts are linked.

- At the conclusion of re-reading several favourite texts, organise students into small groups.
- Have students discuss and make connections between the texts.
- Provide time for students to individually record the titles of the selected texts.

• Direct students to draw lines between the text titles and record any connections they have made.
• Invite students to share connections.

Adaptations:

Once students are familiar with creating Linking Lines between written texts, they can be challenged to create Linking Lines to well-known movies, TV shows or websites.

5 What's in a Text?

The foci of the What's in a Text? activity are to assist students to make connections to other texts and to draw upon their knowledge of the organisation and structure of particular text forms.

What's in a Text works successfully when students work in small groups and use brainstorming to record as much information as possible.

• Provide small groups with a common text.
• Provide a list of questions about the selected text form to stimulate discussion and activate prior knowledge.
• Have students answer the questions.
• Provide students with ample time to read the text.
• Encourage students to discuss the text-to-text connections made during reading. Discussions can include how the selected text form was similar to or different from other texts.

What's in a Text? Questions

What other texts have you read that were <u>fables</u>?
What do you know about <u>fables</u>?
What sort of words or phrases do you expect to find in a <u>fable</u>?
How do <u>fables</u> usually begin?
How do <u>fables</u> usually end?
What types of characters are usually found in a <u>fable</u>?

Use what you already know about <u>fables</u>, the cover, title and illustrations to make a prediction about what this text is about.

Figure 4.27 What's in a Text? Questions

Adaptations:

The format provided on the CD-ROM can be adapted to be used with any particular text form.

READING STRATEGY: COMPARING

Guided Practice Activities

1 Venn Diagrams

2 Like or Unlike?

3 Just Like

4 Double Entry Journal

1 Venn Diagrams

Completing Venn Diagrams (two or more overlapping circles) allows students to focus on making comparisons between topics, text types, authors, characters, plot and facts. Initially, readers can compare two characters, either from one text or from different texts. As students become familiar with the process, they can compare characters from more than two texts.

- Invite students to compare two characters, e.g. **Town Mouse and Country Mouse**.
- Have students work with partners or in small groups to record things they remember about each character e.g. **character traits, actions, physical appearance**.
- Ask students to examine the two lists to decide which things are common to both characters. Have students transfer this information to the intersecting space on the Venn Diagram.
- Direct students to transfer the remaining information on the list to the appropriate place on the Venn Diagram.
- Provide time for students to discuss the similarities and differences between the characters.

2 Like or Unlike?

Like or Unlike? is an activity that encourages readers to make connections and comparisons between what they know about their world and the way characters or people are represented in a text.

- Select a main character or person from a text. Identify their role, e.g. **"Lui is a teenage girl."**
- Before reading the text, invite students to share what they know about real-life people who fulfil the same role.
- Record responses on a class chart.
- Have students read the text.
- Provide time to discuss how the person or character has been represented in the text. Record these on a class chart.
- Draw students' attention to any differences or similarities between

what they know and how the characters or people may have been represented in text.

• Provide opportunities for students to discuss how the author could change the way the character or person was represented and the impact this would have on the text.

3 Just Like

Just Like (Hoyt 1999) is an activity that encourages readers to make connections and comparisons between a selected character and characters from other texts or people they know in real life.

• After reading a text, direct students to select a main character or person.

• Invite students to brainstorm all the character traits related to their chosen person or character. These character traits should be listed in Column 1 of the Just Like format.

• Encourage students to make comparisons between the characters and themselves, other characters in different texts or people they know. This involves students thinking more specifically about the similarities and differences between the characters and these other groups.

• Direct students to complete the table.

• Provide opportunities for students to share their comparisons.

Just Like			
Character *Grandfather*		Text *Something from Nothing - Phoebe Gilman*	
Character Traits	Like Myself	Like Someone I Know	Reminds me of Another Character
clever	-	My teacher	Harry Potter
hard working	✓	Scott	The Little Red Hen
kind	✓	Mary Lou	Snow White
friendly	✓	Jane (our neighbour)	Wilfred Gordon MacDonald Partridge

Figure 4.28 Student Sample Just Like

4 Double Entry Journal

The use of a Double Entry Journal encourages students to consider the similarities and differences within and across texts. Double Entry Journals could be used to record and make comparisons between the text and the connections that have been made during reading.

• Provide students with a Double Entry Journal Format.

- Provide time for students to read the selected text.
- Direct students to record key events from the text and to note any connections they make. Similarities and differences can also be noted about their connections, e.g. **This storyline reminds of the previous book I read except the main character was a female not a male.**
- Provide time for students to share their connections and comparisons.

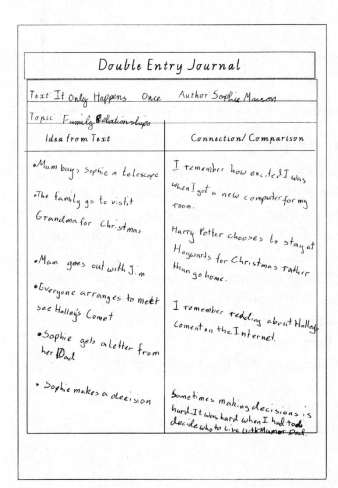

Figure 4.29 Student Sample Double Entry Journal

READING STRATEGY: INFERRING

Guided Practice Activities

1 Character Self-Portrait

2 Interviews

3 Rating Scales

4 Report Card

5 What's My Point of View?

6 Developing Dialogue

1 Character Self-Portrait

Creating a Character Self-Portrait provides readers with an opportunity to combine information from the text with their prior knowledge. While completing a character profile, students discuss inferences and opinions about characters and listen to the points of view and interpretations of others.

• Construct a Character Self-Portrait framework consisting of appropriate sentence stems that relate to the text. It is essential to vary the framework for different texts.

• Jointly select a character from the text.

• Have the students discuss the character then complete the sentence stems.

• Record student responses on the framework.

• Invite students to refer to the text to support their responses for each completed stem.

Adaptations:

Teachers can vary the framework so it is suitable for a wide range of texts. The Character Self-Portrait activity can also be used successfully with informational texts such as biographies or historical accounts.

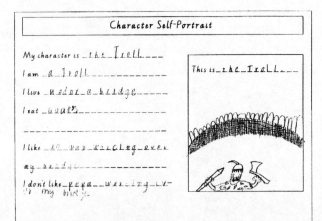

Figure 4.30 Student Sample Character Self-Portrait

2 Interviews

The activity Interviews involves students role-playing a question-and-answer situation. One student takes on the role of a character or person while the other student asks the questions. Participating in Interviews allows readers to make inferences about a character's or person's actions and behaviours.

Students role-playing the character or person are required to answer questions asked by their partner. Students will make their own inferences, draw conclusions and make connections to respond to questions and present their own interpretations of the text.

Students conducting the interviews need to create questions that will elicit personal interpretations of the text. It is important to model the types of questions that will help students to focus on finding out about the character's or person's actions, feelings, and behaviours.

- Organise the students into pairs. Have students select a character or person from a previously read text.
- Have students negotiate who will be the character or person and who will be the interviewer.
- Have the pairs work together to develop appropriate questions.
- Provide time for the students to conduct their interviews.
- Invite the students to share some interviews with the whole class.
- At the conclusion of each shared interview, invite the students to discuss which parts of the text influenced the questions and answers.

Interview Questions for the girl in *My Mama Had a Dancing Heart*

Where was your dad during your life?
What was your favourite thing you did with your mama?
If your mama was around today, what would you say to her?

Figure 4.31 Sample Interview Questions for *My Mama Had a Dancing Heart*

3 Rating Scales

Completing a Rating Scale encourages readers to discuss and assess the qualities displayed by characters or people in texts, and to justify their assessments in small group or whole class discussions. Rating Scales provide students with the opportunity to share their feelings about different characters or people from a text. Providing time for discussion helps readers to relate attributes and actions of characters to their own experiences.

When first creating Rating Scales, students will often select traits that closely relate to the action of the characters or people.

- Provide time for students to read the selected text.
- Invite small groups of students to select a main character or person to 'rate'.
- Direct students to discuss the character or person and list a range of different traits, e.g. **neat, bossy, friendly, helpful**. Discuss and list the opposite of each trait. A class-generated bank of traits written on a chart allows students to work without assistance.
- Provide time for students to discuss the selected character or person and their traits, listening to a range of viewpoints. Students make inferences about the character or person and rate them on the scale.
- Encourage students to refer to the text to validate their ratings, e.g. **I rated Francesco as very smart because he recovered the stolen gold by tricking the thief.** Record this justification in the space provided on the framework.
- Encourage students to rate and compare other characters or people from the text.

Adaptations:

Make ratings at three different points in the text. The three points may be the beginning, mid-point and end of the text. These can be recorded on different grids or on the same grid. Discussions could focus on why the rating has changed.

Consider the rating of a character from the perspective of another character in the text, e.g. **from the perspective of the main character's brother, best friend or mother.**

Character Rating Scale						
TEXT: The day my Bum went AUTHOR: Andy Griffiths CHARACTER: Zack Psycho						
	Very	Quite	Neither/Both No Information	Quite	Very	
Cowardly				✓		Brave
Justification: He is brave but is afraid of some things						
Bad				✓		Good
Justification: He saves the world						
friendly	✓					mean
Justification: He makes friends with everyone.						
active		✓				Lazy
Justification: He travels along way.						
frail				✓		strong
Justification: He lifts fuel cans.						

Figure 4.32 Student Sample Character Rating Scale

4 Report Card

Report Card is an activity where students prepare a traditional school report card for a selected character or person. Students are required to determine the 'appropriate' subject areas, assign a grade and make a comment about the character or person based on the information obtained and inferred from the text.

The subjects can be set by the teacher or brainstormed by the students after a reading of the text. The grading scale can also be set by the teacher or decided on by the students. If appropriate, the school's current report card grading scale could be used

- Provide time for students to read the chosen text and select a character or person, e.g. **Little Red Hen, Dan the Fire Fighter**.
- Have students brainstorm a list of subjects relevant to the character or person, e.g. **cooking, making friends, fighting fires, driving**.
- Invite students to record the subjects in the space provided on the report card format.
- For each subject, the students can decide on a grade and record a comment to support their grade, e.g. **Cooking - A -The Little Red Hen makes a great loaf.**

Adaptation:

Students can grade the chosen character from the perspective of a different character, e.g. **Little Red Hen could be graded from the perspective of a farmyard friend.**

5 What's My Point of View?

Inviting students to discuss events from a text from different points of view stimulates students to make inferences, judgements and build a deeper understanding of actions and behaviour. Retelling the known text from a different perspective can follow group discussions.

- Provide time for students to read a chosen text.
- As a whole class, students can identify and list four or five key events from the text.
- Allocate a character from the text to each small group, e.g. **Mother, younger brother, next-door neighbour**. Encourage students to discuss the key events and actions of characters from the allocated character's point of view.
- Organise students to form new small groups so each character is represented in the new group, e.g. **a mother, a young brother, a next-door neighbour**.
- Encourage students to share their character's point of view about the key events listed.

6 Developing Dialogue

Developing Dialogue is an oral activity that involves students working in pairs to create the dialogue of two characters or people at a particular time. Through the use of the Developing Dialogue activity, readers are encouraged to make inferences. Students are encouraged to make their own interpretations of a text and to consider that others may have different interpretations.

Developing Dialogue works well with literary texts. Once students are familiar with the activity, it can also be applied to informational texts.

- Organise students into pairs. Each pair can then select two characters or people and a particular event from a familiar text.
- Provide time for students to discuss the characters or people and what they would be saying.
- Direct students to create and practise their improvised dialogue. If necessary, have students record key words to use as a memory aid when presenting their dialogue.
- Select several pairs to share their dialogue with the class.
- Students can discuss how and why the dialogues varied.

READING STRATEGY: SYNTHESISING

Guided Practice Activities

1 Turn on the Lights
2 Plot Profile
3 Great Debate
4 Synthesis Journal

1 Turn on the Lights

Turn on the Lights provides students with the opportunity to consciously piece together elements of a text to assist overall comprehension. During reading, students recall and record any information from a text that helps clarify meaning and/or has a significant impact on their understanding thus *Turning on the Lights!*

- Direct students to use the format provided to make jottings (words or pictures) at self-determined points as they read the text.
- Encourage students to be consciously aware of the times when 'pieces come together' for them during the reading. At each of these times, students record the information that is significant in

helping them to monitor and clarify meaning. These are the
AH HA! moments that all readers have during reading.

• Provide an opportunity for students to share and compare their
Turn on the Lights jottings and their understanding of the text,
either in small groups or with a partner.

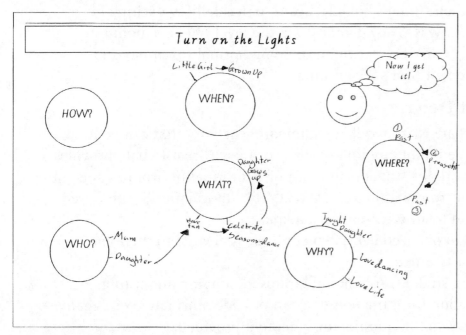

Figure 4.33 Student Sample Turn on the Lights

2 Plot Profile

A Plot Profile format provides a framework for students to
determine the main events of a story. They can then synthesise
the information and rate the excitement level of each event.

• After reading and re-reading a text, have students brainstorm and
list the main events in order.

• Provide time for small groups of students to consider each event
and determine its level of excitement. The excitement level can
then be plotted onto the grid to create a profile of the plot.

• Invite students to summarise the excitement levels of each event
in the text.

• Encourage groups to compare their profiles.

Adaptations:

Plot Profiles can be created during the process of reading a text.
Main events can be recorded as they occur.

After several profiles have been created, note and discuss
similarities and differences in the various profiles. This could
involve comparing profiles from the same author or across similar
text forms.

- Have the students brainstorm the main events. Record each main event onto a separate card.
- Allocate each card to individual students.
- Invite the students to line up in the order of the events as they occurred in the text.
- Jointly re-read each event to check for sequence.
- Invite each student holding a card to decide how exciting his or her event was. They demonstrate the level of excitement by standing tall (very exciting), standing normal (exciting) and sitting down (not very exciting).

3 Great Debate

Great Debate is an excellent culminating activity that can be used at the completion of any unit of study or topic. Great Debate provides a framework for students to synthesise information from a range of sources or from within a single text. This information is then used to respond to an open-ended statement.

- Create an open-ended statement directly related to the topic of study or to a text.
- Organise students to work in groups identifying and listing information from the text that can provide affirmative or negative responses to the question or statement provided.
- Invite individual students to then create a personal position statement. They can also include justifications about the statement.
- Provide time for students to share and compare personal position statements. The sharing of statements allows students to draw conclusions and consider different points of view.

4 Synthesis Journal

A Synthesis Journal (McAlexander & Burrell 1996) provides a framework for students to use when synthesising information about a topic collected from various sources, possibly representing a range of perspectives. By completing a Synthesis Journal, readers are able to develop a greater understanding of how authors use information to suit different purposes and audiences.

Synthesising is a complex process that involves working with information from several sources. This will need to be modelled many times before students can independently create their own journal.

- Invite students to select a topic.
- Have students begin gathering information from a variety of sources, e.g. **texts, a video, a guest speaker ('author says'), classmates, the teacher and/or personal experiences**.

- Invite students to record key information from each source onto the Synthesis Journal framework.
- Direct students to review key information from each source and create a synthesis of the ideas presented. Encourage students to consider the different perspectives presented.

Synthesis Journal			
Source 1: _____	Source 2: _____	Source 3: _____	Source 4: _____
My Synthesis			

Figure 4.34 Sample Synthesis Journal Format

READING STRATEGY: CREATING IMAGES

Guided Practice Activities

1 **Picture This!**
2 **Sensory Chart**
3 **Post Your Senses**
4 **Changing Images**
5 **Open Mind Portrait**
6 **Information Images**

1 Picture This!

Picture This! is an activity that allows students to practise the comprehension strategy of creating images. After listening to a text but not viewing any illustrations, students are invited to create a visual representation of a part of the text.

- Select a section of text that contains a well-described setting and has a variety of characters.
- Read the selection to the students. Ensure students do not see any visual information.
- Direct students to select a character and an event in the text. Provide time for students to create a visual representation of their interpretation.

- If appropriate, encourage students to add sound effects.
- Organise students to share and compare their images. Encourage students to provide reasons for the images they have created.

2 Sensory Chart

The use of a Sensory Chart provides students with an opportunity to 'see', 'feel' and 'hear' the characters, setting or events of the text. This helps the text come alive and support students' interpretations. The charts can be completed on an individual basis but works most effectively when created with a partner.

- Provide time for pairs to read a self-selected section of a text.
- At the end of the reading, encourage students to work individually to record, pictorially or using key words, what the text so far *Looks Like*, *Feels Like* or *Sounds Like*.
- Encourage students to share and compare their images. The opportunity to discuss their images through sharing and comparing is important.
- Direct students to repeat the process for the next self-selected section of the text.

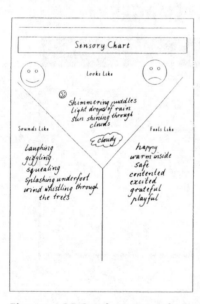

Figure 4.35 Student Sample Sensory Chart

3 Post Your Senses

Post Your Senses is an activity that helps students develop an awareness of creating images to aid comprehension. Post Your Senses involves students recording brief notes or sketches about the images they form as they read a text.

- Provide students with stick-on notes to be used during reading.
- Invite students to place stick-on notes on the text in places where they think of a strong image (visual, auditory, olfactory, kinesthetic or emotional).

- Direct students to make brief notes or sketches about each image.
- Provide time for students to share their images with others. Encourage students to discuss how the images helped them to understand the text.

4 Changing Images

Completing a Changing Images (Miller 2002) activity helps students to understand that mental images evolve and change as more and more information is gathered from a text and new interpretations are developed. Images may also change as a result of sharing with other readers.

- Select a text to read aloud to students. Do not share any illustrations with the students at this time.
- Stop at a selected place in the text. On the format provided, invite students to sketch or write about their mental image in Box 1—*My First Image*.
- Organise students into pairs to discuss and share their mental images.
- Students can add to or re-create their images after conferring with their partners.
- Continue reading aloud to another selected point in the text.
- Allow enough time for students to add to or re-create their images.
- Invite students to reconsider their images at the end of the text.

Figure 4.36 Student Sample Changing Images

5 Open Mind Portrait

Creating Open Mind Portrait (Tompkins 2001) provides students with the opportunity to create not only visual images but emotional images of selected characters in texts. Students are invited to create a portrait of a character and to then record key words to describe the character's thoughts and feelings.

- After reading a text, direct students to fold a large blank sheet of paper in half.
- On one half of the sheet, invite students to select then draw a portrait of a character from their text.
- Direct students to trace the outline of the portrait onto the other half of the sheet. No facial details should be included in this second drawing.
- Invite students to record words or pictures onto the portrait that describes the feelings and thoughts of their chosen character.
- Provide time for students to share their portraits and descriptive words with each other, explaining reasons for their choices.

Adaptations:

Open Mind Portraits activity can be used not only with literary texts but also with informational texts such as biographies or historical accounts.

6 Information Images

It is important that students practise creating images when reading informational texts as well as literary texts. The Information Images activity encourages students to consider visual images when reading informational texts such as subject specific text books, e.g. **science**.

- After reading a section of an informational text, invite students to work in small groups to create images that represent the key information.
- Provide students with large sheets of paper to create the images so posters can be displayed.
- Encourage students to represent the information as two different images.
- Provide time for small groups to share and explain their images with the whole class.

READING STRATEGY: SELF-QUESTIONING

Guided Practice Activities

1 **Clouds of Wonder**
2 **Stop-and-Think Cards**
3 **BDA Questions**
4 **Written Conversation**

1 Clouds of Wonder

It is important that readers be actively thinking during the process of reading. Students can be encouraged to think about characters, events, settings, actions, problems or solutions presented in a text and to generate personal questions that evolve as they read. The use of a Clouds of Wonder framework promotes this type of active thinking.

- Have pairs of students read a section of a text together, e.g. **one page, two paragraphs.**
- Encourage students to reflect on this section and generate 'I wonder …' questions.
- Have students record their questions on their individual Clouds of Wonder sheet.
- Have students share and discuss their 'I wonder …' questions.
- Provide time for students to continue the process to the end of the text, stopping at various points to generate, share and discuss questions.

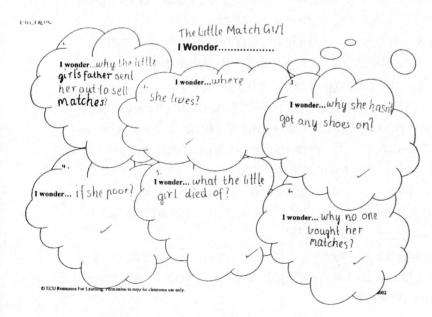

Figure 4.37 Student Sample Clouds of Wonder

2 Stop-and-Think Cards

Effective readers constantly ask themselves questions as a way of monitoring their comprehension. Stop and Think is a simple activity that encourages students to practise pausing at different times during the reading of a text. Stop-and-Think cards placed in self-selected places throughout the text encourage students to use the pauses to ask themselves simple questions and to reflect on their level of understanding.

- Provide time for students to identify random places in a text to *stop and think*.
- Have students mark each place with a Stop-and-Think card.
- Have students identify at least three places in the text.
- Direct students to read the text, stopping to reflect on questions listed on the Stop-and-Think card.

Stop-and-Think Card

Do I understand what that was about?

Were there any parts I did not understand?

Could I explain what I have just read to someone else?

What might the next part be about?

Are there any questions I need to have answered?

Congratulations! Read ON!

Figure 4.38 Stop-and-Think Card

3 BDA Questions

BDA Question sheets are a way of encouraging students to practise generating questions before, during and after reading. Generating questions helps students to set a clear purpose for their reading, predict information and make connections to what they already know. This assists students' overall comprehension.

- Organise students to work with a partner to generate questions before reading a text. Headings and subheadings are a useful aid for generating questions. Questions can be recorded in the Before Reading Column on the format provided.
- Direct students to begin reading, scanning for information to answer their initial questions. Any answers to questions can be recorded in the same column.
- Encourage students to generate any further questions as they read, recording them in the During Reading Column. Answers can be recorded when found.

- At the end of reading, partners work together to generate any further questions they have about the topic. These questions can be used as discussion starters for further small group sharing sessions or individual research.

BDA Questions		
BEFORE READING	DURING READING	AFTER READING
What are the most dangerous spiders? How do spiders make webs? Have people died from a spider bite?	How many different types of spiders are there? Why do spiders need 8 eyes?	Why are so many people scared of spiders?

Figure 4.39 Student Sample BDA Questions

4 Written Conversation

Readers benefit from opportunities to discuss their questions and interpretation of a text with a partner. Written Conversations allow students to use writing to explore their thoughts and questions about a text.

- Organise students to work with a partner to read the same text, chapter or passage.
- After reading, provide time for students to 'converse' about the text in a written form (no talking allowed). Partners take turns writing back and forth on the same sheet of paper.
- Encourage students to consider recording thoughts as well as asking each other questions about what and why things may have happened in the text.
- Provide time for partners to share their written conversations with other groups.

READING STRATEGY: SKIMMING

Guided Practice Activities

1 **Picture Flick**
2 **Graphic Overlays**
3 **Sneak Preview**

1 Picture Flick

Picture Flick is an activity that replicates what many efficient readers do before they read a text that contains illustrations. It is often a natural process to skim through the illustrations to get a sense of the contents, characters or setting. Taking a brief look at illustrations in a text can help prepare readers for the text as well as stimulating predictions and connections.

• Encourage students to use the following Picture Flick procedure prior to independent reading.
  – Look at the front cover and the title of the text.
  – Skim through the text, browsing at the illustrations.
  – After looking through the whole text, 'predict the story'.
    Ask: What do you think is going to happen in the text?
• Provide time for students to read the text.
• Have students discuss and make comparisons between their predictions and what actually happened in the text.
• Provide time for students to share how skimming a text helped with comprehension of the text.

Adaptation:

Picture Flick can be done with the whole class when using enlarged texts such as big books.

2 Graphic Overlays

Graphic Overlays provide students with an opportunity to build their knowledge of text organisation. It is sometimes difficult for readers to follow texts that include pictures, diagrams, tables, graphs, text and photographs. Some informational texts are organised into columns or print is placed alongside unrelated graphics. This organisation of text may hinder comprehension.

The creation of a Graphic Overlay, through skimming a text prior to reading, provides students with a clear visual outline of how and where information is located in the text.

- Provide students with non-permanent markers and transparent overlays, e.g. **overheads, plastic sheeting, tracing paper.**
- Have students place the transparent sheeting over the page/s of the text.
- Ask students to then create a visual representation of the layout or organisation of the page. Boxes are drawn to represent chunks of text, diagrams, headings, labels or photographs.
- Direct students to label each box, describing what it represents, e.g. **text, subheading, photograph, caption.**
- Provide opportunities for students to use the Graphic Overlay to explain the layout of the text to a partner.
- Direct students to use the overlay to identify the parts of the text that may assist them achieve their reading purpose.

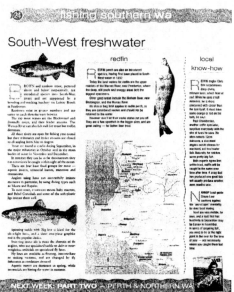

Figure 4.40a Sample Text

Figure 4.40b Student Sample Graphic Overlay

3 Sneak Preview

Completing a Sneak Preview sheet encourages students to skim a text before they begin reading. This will motivate students to build interest in the text and will assist with comprehension. Students can skim to identify particular features such as the contents page, cover, back cover blurb, end pages, information about the author, illustrations and chapter headings.

- Invite students to explore the organisation and contents of their text prior to reading.
- Provide time for students to complete the Sneak Preview sheet.
- Encourage students to share what they discovered with a partner or in small groups.

- Provide time for students to read the text, encouraging them to use the information gathered through skimming.
- Provide time for students to reflect on what information was most useful to assist comprehension.

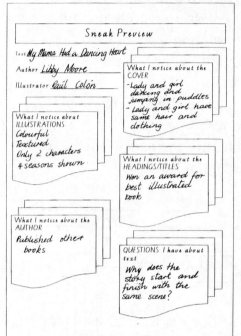

Figure 4.41 Student Sample Sneak Preview

READING STRATEGY: SCANNING

Guided Practice Activities

1 **Hunt the Text Challenge**
2 **Beat the Buzzer Quiz**
3 **Retrieval Charts**
4 **Interesting Words Chart**

1 Hunt the Text Challenge

Hunt the Text Challenge is a type of quiz that provides students with the opportunity to scan text to locate specific information. Challenges can be presented one at a time and involve the students in scanning features used to organise text such as the index, contents page, illustrations, headings and subheadings. Students can then answer the questions provided.

- Prepare a variety of challenge cards containing questions based on a selected text. Ensure that the challenges encourage students to scan the text to locate specific information such as page numbers, particular details, a certain illustration or table, a statistic, a specific heading or subheading, a chapter title or an answer to a question.

- Create a game-like situation by randomly drawing challenge cards from a box.
- Read the card aloud and challenge the students to locate the information.
- Direct students to use a certain sign to indicate they have found the answer, e.g. **hand up**.

Adaptation:

Students could work in small groups with one student as the quiz person, and the others responding to the challenges presented.

2 Beat the Buzzer Quiz

This activity is a fun way of helping students to practise scanning text to locate specific details. Responses to quiz questions can be substantiated by students providing a reference for information located in the text, e.g. **Page 3, second paragraph**.

- After reading a text, direct students to work in pairs to create quiz questions for other students using the text.
- Provide time for questions to be recorded onto cards. Collect cards.
- Organise students into two teams.
- Select a question and read it to the whole class. Challenge the teams to provide the answer as well as a specific reference to a page and paragraph in the text that substantiates their answer.
- A point can be scored for the fastest team that responds to each question.

3 Retrieval Charts

A Retrieval Chart enables students to record information about a number of categories or topics so they can make comparisons. To create a Retrieval Chart, students scan a text to extract important information so they can make generalisations.

- Create headings for the Retrieval Chart based on the type of information to be gathered.
- Introduce these headings to the students.
- Allow students time to read the text/s.
- Provide time for students to scan the text/s so they can identify relevant information.
- Allocate time for students to record the information they have found onto the Retrieval Chart.
- Discuss with students the similarities and differences in the categories.

Adaptations:

Retrieval Charts can be completed using key words or pictorial representations.

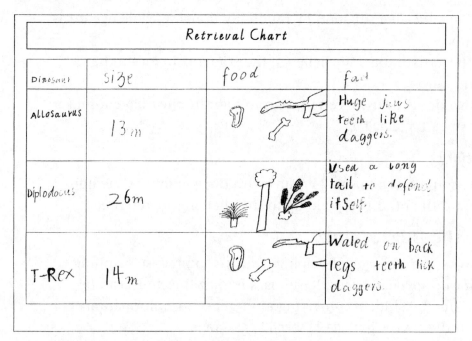

Figure 4.42 Student Sample Pictorial Retrieval Chart

4 Interesting Words Chart

Interesting Words Chart (Morris, A. and Stewart-Dore, N. 1984)
is an activity that is used to clarify new or unknown vocabulary,
particularly in informational texts. Students skim for context clues
in the text, use what they already know and reference materials
such as dictionaries to work out word meanings before, during
and/or after reading.

• Direct students to skim the text. Have them highlight any new
  vocabulary or words where the meaning is unknown or unclear.

• Ask students to share any new words. If students seem hesitant to
  respond, prompt the students with pre-selected words, e.g. **What
  about the word 'molten'? Does anyone know what that word means?**

• Enter suggested words onto the Interesting Words Chart and
  include a page and/or paragraph reference.

• Have students read the text looking for contextual clues that
  might suggest a meaning for the word. If contextual clues are
  found, have the students complete the 'Help Given in the Text'
  column. If no contextual clues are found but the student can infer
  the meaning, they can write this meaning in the 'Your
  Explanation' column.

• If the meaning is still not determined, direct students to a glossary,
  dictionary or any other reference source. The correct meaning is
  then recorded in the final column.

• As words often have several meanings, students need to be sure
  they have selected the correct meaning for the text. To confirm

their understanding of the word, have students re-read the section of text, using the meaning they have sourced, to make sure that the text makes sense.
- Have students re-read the text in its entirety.

Interesting Words Chart				
WORD	PAGE and/or PARAGRAPH	ANY HELP GIVEN IN THE TEXT	YOUR EXPLANATION	MEANING FROM ANOTHER SOURCE
mortality	22 para 3	Yes - bracket explanation	deaths	
morbidity	22 para 3	Yes - bracket explanation	illness	
malaria	24 para 1 5 6	Pg 23 para. on diseases Pg 24 cholera + malaria are diseases (that) ... (stated)	Tropical disease spread by mosquito	
cholera	24 para 1 3 4	Text - cholera + malaria are diseases .... (stated)	disease affecting intestines	
ecosystem	25 last paragraph		Not sure? I think to do with lakes + swamps	Dictionary - system involving interactions between community + its non-living environment
endemic	25 para 2	Yes - bracket explanation	found regularly	

4.43 Student Sample Interesting Words Chart

READING STRATEGY: DETERMINING IMPORTANCE

Guided Practice Activities

1 What's Your Story?
2 Famous Five-Key Word Search
3 Very Important Points (VIPs)
4 Main Idea Pyramid

1 What's Your Story?

The What's Your Story? framework distils the key elements of a narrative text into a simple diagram. Completing this activity requires students to identify important information. It also promotes awareness of how knowing the organisation of a narrative text aids comprehension. What's Your Story? also helps students to make connections between different parts of a narrative.
- Provide time for students to read the selected text.
- Direct students to work in small groups to locate and record key information under each category on the sheet.
- Provide the opportunity for students to share and compare information recorded.

Adaptations:

What's Your Story sheets can be adapted to suit a variety of other texts. Once students have completed several What's Your Story? sheets, these can be used to look for patterns and make comparisons across different texts.

Figure 4.44 Student Sample What's Your Story?

2 Famous Five-Key Word Search

Involving students in Key Word Searches is an effective way of helping them to extract important information from texts. The success of strategies such as summarising and paraphrasing depends on students' ability to select appropriate key words. The process of selecting key words will need to be modelled many times starting with single sentences and moving into more complex and lengthy examples. Once students have worked in this context, the Famous Five-Key framework can be used independently.

- Provide time for students to read the selected passage and identify possible key words during reading. These may be recorded on stick-on notes.
- At the conclusion of reading, direct the students to re-read the possible key words and select the *famous five* key words.
- Invite students to record their famous fives onto the format.
- Provide time for students to share their key words in small groups. They can discuss and compare their selections.
- Direct students to use the key words as a stimulus to create their own sentences about the text.

3 Very Important Points (VIPs)

VIPs (Hoyt 2002) is a simple activity that encourages students to identify important information in a text. Students create a fringe of stick-on note strips that are used to mark identified sections of a text that contain very important points. The use of the stick-on note strips allows students some flexibility in their final choice of VIPs.

- Allocate a certain number of strips. Limiting the number of strips to be used helps students to focus.
- Provide time for students to create their fringe of strips.
- Provide time for students to read the text and place their strips on what they consider to be VIPs. These should be places in the text that are significant to the overall meaning of the text.
- Provide time for students to share and compare their VIPs and verify their selections.

4 Main Idea Pyramid

The Main Idea Pyramid is a graphic organiser that helps students to determine and record important information in a paragraph or an entire text. The pyramid activity helps to show the relationship between supporting details and the main idea. Paragraphs with clear topic sentences and simple lists are ideal texts when first using Main Idea Pyramids.

- After reading a text or sections of a text, students brainstorm important facts. Encourage students to refer to the text if necessary.
- Have students record facts on cards or notes so they can be moved.
- When the brainstorming process is complete, direct students to group their cards or notes into general sub-topics. Place these groups of cards or notes at the base of the pyramid.
- Direct students to re-read the combination of words or phrases in each group and record a main idea statement for each one. These statements form the second level of the pyramid.
- Direct students to then use all the information at the second level to create a main idea of the text. This forms the top level of the pyramid.

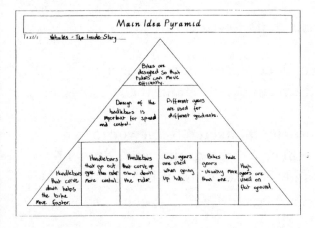

Figure 4.45 Sample Main Idea Pyramid

READING STRATEGIES: SUMMARISING AND PARAPHRASING

Guided Practice Activities

1 Oral Summaries
2 Reciprocal Retells
3 Main Idea Sort
4 Newspaper Report
5 66 Words

1 Oral Summaries

Oral Summaries is an activity that helps students to monitor their own comprehension and to substantiate their ideas through summarising.

• Allocate students to work in small groups using the same text.
• Direct students to read a specified section of the text silently or aloud.
• Invite small groups to collaboratively summarise what has happened so far in the text. Encourage discussion and substantiation.
• Direct students to read the next specified section, stopping to repeat the process of creating a group summary.

2 Reciprocal Retells

The ability to summarise and paraphrase important information from a text requires students to be able to strip away extraneous information. This requires practice and modelling. Reciprocal Retells allows students to extract important information to use it as a basis for retelling.

• After reading a text, direct students to work in small groups to brainstorm main events.
• Invite each student in the small group to select one of the main events.
• Using the framework provided, direct each student to work individually to elicit and list the main details about their selected event.
• Provide time for students to use the completed framework as a guide to prepare a reciprocal oral or written group retell. Student A (Event 1) begins the retell and then passes it on to Student B

(Event 2) to continue. This process is continued for each student and therefore each main event.

- Encourage small groups to share their Reciprocal Retells with the whole class.

Adaptation:

By changing the Text Organisation heading, the Reciprocal Retell framework can be adapted to suit a variety of literary texts.

3 Main Idea Sort

Main Idea Sort activity enables students to identify key words and phrases to create summaries. The Main Idea Sort is an excellent activity to use with informational texts.

- Identify key words, phrases and headings that are necessary for understanding the concepts of the topic in a selected text.
- Record key words and phrases randomly on a grid.
- Have students read the text.
- After reading, students can cut up the grid into small cards.
- Invite students to arrange words, phrases and headings to show their relationship, thereby forming an outline of the text.
- Direct students to work in pairs, using the key words and phrases to create a summary of the text.

4 Newspaper Report

Creating Newspaper Reports from texts provides an opportunity for students to summarise and paraphrase the main ideas into a new form. A grasp of the organisation, purpose, structure and features of a newspaper report is a pre-requisite for the completion of this activity.

- Provide time for students to read a text and discuss the main events.
- Direct students to work together to re-create an important event as if it was being reported in the newspaper. The following features can be included:
  - headline to capture attention
  - date and place
  - lead sentence to encourage the reader to read on
  - details such as who, what, why, how and when
  - conclusion
  - picture.
- Provide time for students to present and compare their newspaper reports.

5 66 Words

The 66 Words is a framework that can be used to record the key events or themes of a text. Students are challenged to read a text and create a summary in sixty-six words or less. By providing students with a grid with sixty-six rectangles, the focus is on succinct text rather than the exact number of words.

• Have students individually write their 66 Word summary in sentences.

• Organise students into small groups. Each small group merges individual ideas to create a single summary in sixty-six words or less. If consensus is difficult, each group member may have a turn at making the final decision about at least one sentence.

• Have groups share their 66 Word summary. Discuss what was included, what was left out and why.

Bridge	to	Terabithia	is	a	story	of	a
journey	toward	relation-ships	and	imaginatio	It	explores	the
life	of	a	boy	called	Jess	who	lives
with	many	sisters	and	his	family	in	a
small	rural	community	Jess	develops	an	unlikely	friendship
with	a	girl	called	Leslie,	who	develops	in
Jess	the	strength	to	cope	with	a	tragedy.
This	tragedy	develops	a	bond	between	Jess	and
his	dad.						

66 Words

Text *Bridge to Terabithia* Author *Katherine Patterson*

Figure 4.46 Student Sample 66 Words

READING STRATEGIES: RE-READING, READING ON, ADJUSTING READING RATE

Guided Practice Activities

No Guided Practice Activities are suggested for these strategies. It is recommended that students be encouraged to make use of these strategies during any reading event. The following reading procedures would provide ideal contexts for guiding students to practise re-reading, reading on and adjusting reading rate.

1　Shared Reading

2　Guided Reading

3　Independent Reading

4　Book Discussion Groups

Figure 4.47 Guided Practice Activities

READING STRATEGIES: SOUNDING OUT, CHUNKING, USING ANALOGY, CONSULTING A REFERENCE

Guided Practice Activities

No Guided Practice Activities are suggested for these strategies. It is recommended that students be encouraged to make use of these strategies to identify unknown words during any reading event. The following reading procedures would provide ideal contexts for guiding students to practise sounding out, chunking, using analogy and consulting a reference.

1　Shared Reading

2　Guided Reading

3　Independent Reading

For further Guided Practice Activities, see *First Steps Reading Map of Development Second Edition*, Chapters 4–8: Conventions Substrand.

Figure 4.48 Guided Practice Activities

A Record of Strategies Introduced

Comprehension and word identification strategies can and must be taught. Throughout this chapter, many different strategies have been explored that are used by efficient readers. The *Gradual Release of Responsibility Model* is an effective way of teaching these strategies.

The following framework provides a way of tracking strategies that have been introduced to students. The framework also provides space so teachers can monitor the recursive use of modelling, sharing and guiding to teach the strategies.

Record of Strategies Introduced										
Class: _____ Teacher: _____										
Focus Strategy	Modelling Sessions Conducted				Sharing Sessions Conducted				Guiding Sessions and Guided Practice Activities	Texts Used

Figure 4.49 Record of Strategies Introduced

SECTION 2

Teaching Students to Access and Use Information

What Is the Information Process?

In today's society, more and more information is available so it is essential that schools and teachers prepare students with the skills they need to be able to locate, access, retrieve, process, analyse and utilise information. These skills will enhance the creative and critical thinking of students and set them up to be life-long learners.

The term Information Process is used to describe a sequence of learning processes that students use actively as part of investigations.

Step 1—**Identify** and **define** an investigation
Step 2—**Locate** appropriate resources
Step 3—**Select** and **record** appropriate information
Step 4—**Process** and **organise** the information
Step 5—**Create** and **share** a presentation
Step 6—**Evaluate** the investigation.

Teachers often refer to the Information Process as project work, research assignments, inquiries or investigations. Depending on the type and scope of an investigation, all can be successfully carried out by individuals, pairs or groups of students.

The Information Process remains constant but as students become involved in more challenging investigations, the skills and knowledge they require will become more advanced.

Using the Gradual Release of Responsibility Model (Pearson & Gallagher 1993) ensures that students do not become overloaded. Explicit teaching that incorporates modelling and scaffolded support structures will assist students. Providing students with the time and support needed to develop their knowledge and skills will result in them becoming independent investigators. The teaching of knowledge and skills needs to occur prior to independent application.

Information Process skills can be taught, developed and integrated across all learning areas as these cross-curricular links provide authentic contexts for investigations and real audiences for presentations.

Considerations About Investigations

Investigations need to:
- have a clear purpose and expectations
- have an authentic audience
- be relevant to the student
- allow for individual preferences and ownership
- be planned
- provide opportunities for students to practise and develop skills
- be motivational, flexible and promote engagement
- promote reflection
- have authentic assessment tools
- promote both process and product.

Students need to have a clear understanding of the expectations of an investigation from the outset including the assessment criteria and tools to be used as well as their part in the evaluation process. Therefore, teachers should consider the following questions:
- Do I have a clear purpose for setting the investigation and for the assessment and evaluation processes I will use?
- Have I planned to collect data throughout the investigation as well as at the end?
- What tools will I use to gather data?
- Have I incorporated a collaborative approach in my data collection?
- How will I record the data collected?
- How will I analyse and evaluate the data gathered and incorporate it into my future teaching?

Investigations take time particularly those that are more complex. Some investigations may need to be divided into manageable sections with guidelines. As students investigate, they should be encouraged to develop their own opinions and become autonomous. This may mean that the teacher has to shift away from the more 'traditional' teacher role.

Teachers may find the following formats useful as they work with students during the different stages of the Information Process.
- Sample Investigation Plan—Instructions for Writing Your Imported Animals Investigation
- Sample Parent Letter

Step 1—Identifying and Defining an Investigation

The first step of the Information Process involves identifying and defining the requirements of the investigation. Investigations can be directed by the teacher or negotiated with the student. If the teacher is directing the investigation, then students will need to identify and define both the topic and what they are required to do. If the student has negotiated the investigation, he or she will need to select and define a topic. The chosen investigation should be interesting and relevant to the student, suit a particular audience and be achievable within a specific time frame.

What Students Need to Know

To identify and define an investigation successfully, students will be required to know the following:

• How to Select and Analyse an Investigation Topic

Students who have negotiated their own investigations begin by choosing an aspect to explore and defining the scope of their investigation. It is also beneficial at this stage for students to consider their own interests and what they already know about the topic.

The first task in completing an investigation directed by the teacher is to identify the key words and phrases that define the investigation. Students will then be required to analyse the investigation in terms of the content, the processes they will use and how to organise and present their information.

Regardless of who selected the investigation, it is helpful if students clarify the purpose of the task, know what outcomes need to be demonstrated, determine the audience and check the availability of resources before commencing their investigation.

• How to Create Focus Questions

One way to define the scope of the investigation is to formulate focus questions. Successful focus questions engage the students and head them on a path of discovery thereby providing multiple possibilities for the investigation.

Generating effective questions takes time and practice. Therefore, it is important that teachers work with students to help them develop an understanding of the types of questions to ask and when to ask them.

There are many ways of organising and discussing specific types of questions, e.g. **Bloom's Taxonomy (Bloom 1956) Question Answer**

Relationships (Raphael 1982) Three Level Guides (Herber 1970) or Open and Closed Questions.

Students should understand the nature of the questions and the information that each type of question will elicit. Focus questions may need to be refined or new focus questions created to support the purpose of the task as the investigation proceeds.

• *How to Plan for an Investigation*

Successful investigations require careful management of time and resources. Encourage students to plan so that they follow a logical progression and the investigation is divided into manageable sections. By planning and organising an investigation in this way, it will not become overwhelming, the focus will be retained and reflection and review points can be incorporated throughout the investigation.

Planning an investigation requires students to:
- develop a search plan for possible resources and sources of information
- develop and use planning frameworks.

Teachers can encourage students to organise their time and resources by jointly constructing:
- timetables, calendars and timelines that list due dates for specific tasks
- guides that outline each step of the Information Process.

Teachers can also suggest using organisational aids such as folders or wallets for storing documentation.

Being able to answer the following questions may help students to identify and define an investigation.

Questions for Students

Investigations Directed by Teachers

What is this investigation about?

What do I have to do?

What is the purpose of the investigation?

What do I already know?

What do I want and need to find out?

Have I created focus questions?

What are some key words I could use to search for information?

How will I plan and organise my investigation?

Have I created my plan?

4.50A Questions for Students

Questions for Students

Investigations Negotiated With Students

What would I like to investigate? What am I interested in?

Who is the audience for this investigation?

What do I think will interest them?

What do I already know?

What do I want and need to find out?

Have I created focus questions?

What are some key words I could use to search for information?

How will I plan and organise my investigation?

Have I created my plan?

4.50B Questions for Students

Supporting Students to Identify and Define an Investigation

Teachers can select from the following guided practice activities that will assist students to be able to identify and define an investigation.

1 **Brainstorming**
2 **Card Cluster**
3 **Explosion Chart**
4 **KWL Chart**
5 **Share Your Topic**
6 **Creating Quiz Questions**
7 **5 W's and an H**
8 **Question Web**
9 **Structured Overview**
10 **BDA Questions**

1 Brainstorming

Brainstorming is an activity used to activate students' prior knowledge. When brainstorming, students are required to generate a list of words and phrases about a specific topic. Throughout brainstorming sessions, all suggestions are accepted with 'piggy-backing' of ideas being encouraged.

• Have students work in pairs or groups to generate and record what they already know about the investigation topic.
• Have students categorise the information into sub-topics.
• Once students have finished their brainstorming, they can identify areas where information is lacking. These areas may become the first priority for gathering information.

2 Card Cluster

Creating a Card Cluster is a way of categorising information and is often used to extend a brainstorming session. Clustering involves collating ideas or focus questions by sorting them into categories. This sorting helps students to better plan their investigation.

- Arrange students in groups.
- Distribute blank cards or stick-on notes and a marker pen to each group of students.
- Have students record key words, phrases or questions about their investigation, one idea per card.
- When all the information is recorded on the cards, direct students to place all similar ideas into clusters. Students can explain why they have clustered certain ideas together. Often the explanation can generate a heading for each cluster of cards.
- Students can review each cluster, refining, adding or deleting cards as required.

3 Explosion Chart

Explosion Charts can be used to activate and organise students' prior knowledge and initial questions. An explosion chart starts with the central idea or focus question and as students make associations, they are added to the central idea.

- Have students write the central idea, concept or theme in the middle of a page.
- As students think of ideas and questions, they can write them around the central idea.
- Have students show connections between the ideas, e.g. **cluster information, create radiating lines**.

4 KWL Chart

The use of KWL Charts (Ogle 1986) encourages the activation of the students' prior knowledge of a particular topic and helps students to generate and refine investigation questions.

- Have students brainstorm what they already know about the investigation topic and record it in the K column of the KWL chart.
- Students can list what they want to find out in the W column. This information can be written in question form as it can provide the scope of the investigation.
- Once the investigation has been completed, students can fill in the L column. Any further questions can also be recorded.

K.W.L. Chart			
What I Know	What I Want To Find Out	What I Have Learnt	Questions I Still Have
• biggest of the penguins • black and white • live in the cold • lay eggs	• how big they are • Do they live in Antartica or the Arctic? • how many eggs do they have? • what do they eat? • How do they and the eggs stay warm • how long for a baby to hatch?	• 1.15m tall 40kg • live in Antarctic • lay 1 egg • they don't build nests they keep the egg warm with their bodies • male keeps egg warm female goes for food • 65 days for the egg to hatch • hatch in Spring so they can grow strong for winter • only about half the chicks survive • lay eggs in Winter (not spring like other penguins) • they have a fat layer under their skin to stay warm • 4 layers of feathers for wind and waterproofing • huddle in packs for warmth	• What do the chicks die of? • What does a penguin call sound like? • who are the penguins enemies?

Figure 4.51 Student Sample KWL Chart

5 Share Your Topic

Small group discussions provide an opportunity for students to Share Their Topic/s to activate their prior knowledge, to stimulate critical thinking and learn from peers.

• Form students into small groups. Students can be placed into random groups or according to their investigation topic.

• Provide a focus for the discussion by using statements such as "Today, in your groups, share your three potential investigation topics and obtain feedback from the group" or "Today, in your groups, share your chosen investigation topic, what you have listed as your prior knowledge and possible focus questions and ask the group to contribute any further knowledge or ideas that may assist you."

6 Creating Quiz Questions

Creating Quiz Questions can help students develop effective questions. Effective questions form the basis of successful investigations.

• Provide students with a range of question-and-answer formats, e.g. **game cards, survey or questionnaires**.

• Direct students to identify the different ways questions are structured and analyse the answers, e.g. **multiple choice, finish the sentence, yes or no, full written answer**. Students may also discuss which type of question will best suit a particular context.

• Have students discuss, highlight and analyse the language used in the different questions.

- Provide groups with a section of text and ask them to create a set of questions.
- Have students share and refine questions with another group.
- The students can use the questions to create a quiz session.

7 5W's and an H

The activity 5W's and an H can assist students to generate and refine effective focus questions. Students are challenged to list as many questions related to their investigation as possible under each of the headings on the 5W's and an H format.

- Provide students with a 5W's and an H format.
- Direct students to list as many questions as possible that begin with the given word. Record their questions on the format.
- After listing all possibilities, students can review their questions deleting any that require a limited response. Have students refine any questions that are too general.
- From this revised list, students can number the questions in order of priority. Prioritising will assist with planning and time management.

Five Ws and an H

My Investigation

WHAT DO I WANT TO KNOW? (FOCUS QUESTIONS)

Who?	Who are the people that watch volcanos?
What?	What is the stuff that comes out of volcanoes? What is a volcano made of? What happens when a volcano explodes?
When?	When did the last explosion happen?
Where?	Where did the last explosion happen? Where are the most volcanoes in the world? Where is St Helen's?
Why?	Why do volcanoes explode? Why do some explode + not others?
How?	How hot is a volcano when it explodes? How did volcanoes come to be? How do you know if a volcano is going to explode? How often do they explode?
Check with a Friend (what questions do you think would be most interesting? Do they have any others?)	Does Australia have any volcanoes? Have people died from volcanoes?

Figure 4.52 Student Sample 5W's and an H

8 Question Web

Constructing Question Webs helps students to generate and refine effective focus questions. Students can group questions that relate to similar topics, thereby supplying the subheadings for the investigation.

- Have students brainstorm questions for their investigation using the 5W's and an H format.

- Direct students to review their questions and begin to categorise them into topic groups.
- Have students create a heading for each topic group.
- Once all questions have been allocated, have students review their questions. This may involve deleting, refining or adding questions.

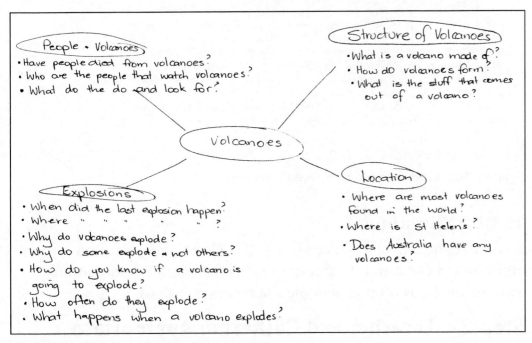

Figure 4.53 Student Sample Question Web

9 Structured Overview

A Structured Overview is a graphic organiser that allows information to be displayed visually showing the relationships between ideas. The Structured Overview provides support for students as they organise their thoughts and ideas for their investigation. The overview can also be used to record and retrieve information at later stages in the investigation. Structured Overviews are usually organised by placing the most important idea or concept at the top followed by the more specific details.

- Have students formulate an overall main idea statement or focus question. This can be written at the top of the Structured Overview.
- In the next level, have students list the potential subheadings or focus questions for each category.
- Under each subheading or focus question, have students list any known information. Students can then generate and write further questions under each subheading.

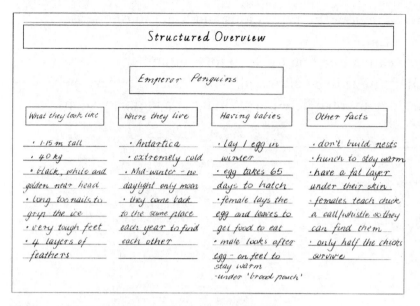

Figure 4.54 Student Sample Structured Overview

10 BDA Questions

(See this book, Chapter 4, Section 1—Teaching Comprehension and Word Identification Strategies) At this stage in the Information Process, the focus is on generating the before questions.

Step 2—Locating and Gathering Appropriate Resources

The second step in the Information Process requires students to locate information using primary and secondary sources. This involves identifying and selecting appropriate resources, locating resources and finding the relevant information within these resources.

Students benefit from being involved in asking, watching, reading and doing at this stage of the process. They may need to modify their search plan as they find new resources, encounter dead ends and gain new insights.

What Students Need to Know

To successfully locate appropriate resources, student will need to know the following:

• *Locating Appropriate Sources of Information*

Students need to have access to a range of resources and sources of information. This range includes access to primary sources of information such as first-hand experiences, simulations, people, services and artefacts and secondary sources of information such as print, non-print and electronic resources.

Using the Library Resource Centre

Students benefit from knowing:
- how the library resource centre is organised, e.g. layout and physical location of resources, the alphabetical and numerical (Dewey) organisational systems
- how the library resource centre accessing systems operate, e.g. catalogues
- how to use the accessing systems effectively
- how to borrow sources
- about the structure of books, e.g. fiction or non fiction, title, author, illustrator, editor, spine, cover, call number, title page, blurb, copyright and publishing details, contents page, index, chapters, dedication, bibliography, glossary, preface, foreword, appendix
- the conventions associated with accessing texts and other resources, e.g. dictionaries and encyclopaedias have guidewords.

Using the Available Technology

Students benefit from knowing how to:
- use equipment, e.g. CD/tape player, computer, microfiche reader, fax machine, television, video/DVD player, film or slide projector, camera, video recorder, telephone
- use search engines, on-line catalogues and databases
- use collaboration tools such as email, discussion lists, forums to elicit and contribute relevant information
- navigate web pages, e.g. using hyperlinks, book marking
- use relevant software.

Conducting Interviews and Surveys

Students will benefit from knowing how to:
- request information using appropriate protocols, e.g. writing explanatory letters, engaging in conversation to set the context for the requested information
- create effective interview or survey questions so they obtain the desired information
- record and collate information from interviews and surveys.

• *Gathering Appropriate Resources*

Students will benefit from knowing how to determine:
- the availability of resources, their ease of use and their readability
- the credibility of the creators of the texts, e.g. checking for credentials, awards, other works, funding from a third party.
- the accuracy, currency and reliability of the texts by referring to publication information, copyright information and edition information.

• *Locating Appropriate Information Within a Resource*

To successfully locate appropriate information within a resource, students will need to know the following:

– how to skim and scan the organisational features of a text, e.g. illustrations, diagrams, graphs, tables, title page, blurb, index, chapters, bibliography, glossary, appendix (See this book, Chapter 3— Conventions).

• *Recording the Resources*

Students will benefit from knowing how to create a bibliography so they can record sources of information and resources using the correct conventions.

Being able to answer the following questions may help students locate and gather appropriate resources.

Questions for Students to Consider

Apart from at school, where else could I go for information?

Which sources and resources are most likely to provide the most reliable information?

How will I access these sources and resources?

Do I know where to find the resources listed on my plan?

Which of the resources will be most readily available and accessible?

Have I considered and checked out a range of resources to include print, non-print and electronic?

Which resources will be most efficient and effective?

Have I previewed the resources I am thinking of using to make sure that I can read and understand them and that they will meet my needs?

Do the resources have useful organisational features so that I can access and retrieve information?

Does it look like the information will answer my questions?

Is it what I want and need?

Have I previewed the resources and the suitability of the information for relevance, currency, reliability, validity and accuracy?

What do I know about the credibility of the authors of these texts?

Have I recorded the resources I want to use so that I can find them again?

Do I need to go back to my original plan and focus questions and make any changes or additions based on my searching?

Have I begun recording my resources?

Figure 4.55 Questions for Students to Consider

Supporting Students to Locate and Gather Appropriate Resources

Teachers can select from the following guided practice activities that will assist students to locate and gather appropriate resources.

1 'Pass That Please'
2 Text Organisational Features Survey
3 Sneak Preview
4 Hunt the Text Challenge
5 Beat the Buzzer Quiz
6 Graphic Overlays
7 Think Sheet
8 BDA Questions

1 'Pass That Please'

The activity 'Pass That Please' is designed to help students practise previewing a text by skimming the organisational features of a text. This activity also highlights the vast range of resources that are available when conducting an investigation.

This activity is most useful when students are working on a teacher-directed investigation as the resources can be located ahead of time.

• Collect a range of resources.
• Arrange students in pairs. The pairs can sit and face each other in an inside/outside circle arrangement.
• Give each student a resource to preview. Provide students with time to preview the resource.
• Have partners take turns to share their findings and comment on the suitability of each text for their investigation. Have students pass the resource on and receive another resource to preview.

2 Text Organisational Features Survey

The activity Text Organisational Features Survey allows students to practise previewing a text to identify organisational features so they can access and use the text.

• Give students a text and a survey form listing a range of organisational features in a text.
• Have students preview the text, noting the organisational features on the survey provided.
• Have students repeat the process with a number of texts. Once the survey has been completed, the collated information can be used to determine which texts will be most suitable for their investigation.

The following activities are explained in detail in this book, Chapter 4, Section 1—Teaching Comprehension and Word Identification Strategies.

3 Sneak Preview
4 Hunt the Text Challenge
5 Beat the Buzzer Quiz
6 Graphic Overlays
7 Think Sheet (Raphael 1982)
8 BDA Questions

At this stage in the Information Process, the focus is on using the questions generated before reading. This will help when skimming and scanning resources.

Step 3—Selecting and Recording Appropriate Information

The third step of the Information Process involves students selecting and recording appropriate information to develop their investigation. At this stage of the Information Process, students may also be critically evaluating the suitability of texts. Students will also need to check the credentials of all the creators of the information.

After the chosen texts and information within the texts have been evaluated, students are required to select and record information that will be appropriate to their investigation. This involves students taking and making notes.

What Students Need to Know

To successfully select and record appropriate resources and information within resources, student will need to know the following:

• *About Accessing Different Text Forms*

At this stage of the Information Process, students benefit from knowing how a text is organised so they can locate and access information. This includes knowledge about:
- text organisation, e.g. **contents, index, sections, headings, subheadings, fact boxes, bolded or italicised wording, bullet points, symbols, key, captions, labels, glossary**
- text structure, e.g. **cause/effect, problem/solution, compare/contrast, listing**
- language features, e.g. **grammatical structures, choice of vocabulary.**

• *About Using Technology*

At this stage of the Information Process, students benefit from knowing how to:
– retrieve information from electronic sources
– reference electronic materials.

• *About Taking and Making Notes*

It is critical that students understand the purpose of note-taking and note-making. The taking and making of notes improves recall of important information, increases the students' understanding between new material and their prior knowledge and refocuses the reader's attention.

Note-taking is recording key information from a text. It serves a number of purposes including expanding knowledge of a topic and organising and summarising content for future reference or use in another task. Notes should be complete, concise and easy to understand to the writer at a later date.

Note-making is recording responses to a text by making notes, comments and questions. Note-making promotes critical thinking as students connect the new information with their prior knowledge.

How to Take and Make Notes

To take effective notes, student benefit from knowing how to:
• select or create appropriate note-taking formats
• create a note-taking plan and personal short cuts
• create appropriate headings and subheadings
• identify key information and record key words from written, visual and oral texts
• identify main idea/s and supporting details
• interpret and retrieve information from text, diagrams, maps, graphs, charts, pictures, photographs, flowcharts and tables
• summarise and paraphrase
• synthesise.

How to Record Information

Students also benefit from knowing how to use a variety of methods for recording information in note form. They assist students to make appropriate connections between information. These methods include:
• making lists
• using sequences, e.g. **flow charts, timelines**

- creating graphic organisers, e.g. **semantic grids, retrieval charts, structured overviews, Venn diagrams, concept maps**
- using two column or three column notes.

• *Determining the Appropriateness of the Information*

At this stage of the Information Process, the students may need to re-evaluate and refine their focus questions based on a preliminary preview of their resources. They can use their focus questions to create possible headings and subheadings to assist when taking notes.

Students benefit from knowing how to determine and evaluate:
– information in the text, e.g. **readability, relevance, organisation**
– devices used by authors to present a particular point of view, e.g. **bias, prejudice, omissions, exaggeration, false claims** (See this book, Chapter 2—Contextual Understanding).

Being able to answer the following questions may help students to select and record appropriate information.

Questions for Students to Consider

Do I know how to locate key information in a text?

Do I know the difference between what is a main idea and what is supporting detail?

Which method will I use to take my notes? What format will I use?

As I made my notes, did I look at all the available information including the illustrations, captions, graphs, maps, tables, diagrams and charts?

Have I compiled my notes from various resources and compared the information from those resources?

Did I remember to make notes (personal questions and responses) as well as just taking notes (summarising the text)?

Have I written my notes in point form and not copied large chunks of information?

Can I understand my notes and could I explain what I have learnt to someone using them?

Have I updated my bibliography by recording all the new resources I have used?

Figure 4.56 Questions for Students to Consider

Supporting Students to Select and Record Appropriate Information

Teachers can select from the following guided practice activities that will assist students to select and record appropriate information.

1 **CWSC (Comprehend, Write, Share, Clarify)**
2 **Take Away**
3 **Pick, Pair, Share**
4 **Visualise and Note-take**
5 **Structured Overview**
6 **KWL Chart (Ogle 1983)**
7 **Oral Summaries**
8 **Post Your Senses**
9 **Information Images**
10 **Retrieval Charts**
11 **Check the Text**
12 **Connecting with the Text**
13 **Famous Five-Key Word Search**
14 **Very Important Points (VIPs)**

1 CWSC (Comprehend, Write, Share, Clarify)

The C.W.S.C. activity promotes active listening and provides students with practice in identifying, extracting and clarifying key information.

- Select an appropriate text. Preview the text and mark any relevant places for students to pause as they complete the activity.
- Have students listen to, view or read the text to gain an overall understanding of it.
- Have students listen to, view or read the text again pausing at the selected places. Ask students to write key information (words or phrases) they have identified.
- Continue in this way until the text is completed and notes have been made for each section.
- Have students work in pairs or small groups to share their notes by comparing and clarifying their information. Encourage students to add or delete information if necessary.
- Combine groups and have the students repeat the process.
- Encourage students to listen to, view or read the text again as a final check.

2 Take Away

Take Away is an activity that helps students to identify key information. Students read a text deleting non-essential words such as pronouns, conjunctions and prepositions. This activity is particularly useful when students are working with electronic texts.

- Lead a discussion about those words that carry the meaning, e.g. **verbs, nouns.**
- Provide students with a text and ask them to read it.
- Direct students to re-read the text, sentence by sentence, deleting all the non-essential words and phrases.
- Have students examine the remaining words. Provide time for students to think about these specific words and reasons why they remain.
- In pairs, have students share and compare their words, discussing why certain words have been deleted or left in.

3 Pick, Pair, Share

The use of underlining or highlighting in the Pair, Pick, Share activity helps students to isolate important information. The activity can also be used to identify redundant information. To complete this activity, students need text that can be underlined or highlighted.

- Select a text, preview it and write some focus questions.
- Provide each student with a copy of the text.
- Direct students to read the whole text.
- Before students read the text again, provide them with a copy of the focus questions.
- Instruct students to re-read the text, highlighting or underlining the words or phrases that answer the focus questions. It may be helpful if students are provided with a maximum number of words that they can highlight or underline in each paragraph or page of text.
- In pairs, students can decide which words are most suitable to answer the focus questions.
- After pairs have decided, they can join another pair to share and compare their words. Students do not have to come to a consensus at this stage but may wish to review their word choices based on their discussion.

4 Visualise and Note-take

The Visualise and Note-take activity involves students in representing concepts and main ideas pictorially. This activity will enhance students' understanding and ability to interpret a text. The choice of text for this activity requires careful consideration as not all texts are suitable.

- Provide students with an oral text or a written text with the illustrations removed.
- Have students listen to or read the text.

- Direct students to re-read the text pausing at relevant places to record a visual representation of their understanding, e.g. **sketch, flow chart, cycle, map, chart**. As students become familiar with this activity, words could be included with the visual representation.
- Have students share their representations with a partner or small group.

5 Structured Overview

See this book, page 179, Chapter 4, Step 1—Identifying and Defining an Investigation, for an explanation.

6 KWL Chart (Ogle 1986)

See this book, page 176, Chapter 4, Step 1—Identifying and Defining an Investigation for an explanation. The focus in this stage of the information process will be completing the L column—What I Have Learnt.

The following activities are explained in detail in this book, Chapter 4, Section 1—Teaching Comprehension and Word Identification Strategies.

- Oral Summaries (see page 166)
- Information Images (see page 154)
- Retrieval Charts (see page 161)
- Check the Text (see page 134)
- Connecting with the Text (see page 137)
- Famous Five–Key Word Search (see page 164)
- Very Important Points (VIPs) (see page 165)

Step 4—Processing and Organising Information

The fourth step of the Information Process requires students to process and organise the information for their investigation. Processing involves analysing and synthesising information that has been retrieved from various sources. Organising involves completing initial drafts, refining and redrafting their writing. It is important that students see this step as creating a learning opportunity for others.

What Students Need to Know

To successfully process and organise information, students will need to know about the following.

• *Text Form Knowledge*

Students need to know about the structure of a text, the organisation and language features of a range of oral, visual and written texts. This knowledge will help them to make decisions about the most appropriate way to organise their information for the investigation.

• *Organising the Information*

Once students have made a decision about which particular text form they will use, they can select or create the appropriate framework to organise the information they have gathered.

At this stage of the Information Process, students need to know about creating a written, visual or oral text as required. Creating a text involves completing a first draft, revising, editing, proofreading and redrafting to finalise the text.

Creating written texts requires students to:
• expand upon their short notes to construct complete sentences
• create sentences that express a complete thought
• sequence their information and the sentences
• construct paragraphs that begin with a topic sentence, provide supporting details in the following sentences and conclude with a summary sentence which links into the next paragraph
• connect ideas from one paragraph to the next and throughout an entire text.
• select language features that will suit the text form, topic and audience
• create effective openings, e.g. **use a leading question, share an anecdote, start with dialogue, lead with an informative statement, use the element of surprise, begin with something that leaves the audience questioning or wondering.**
• create effective endings, e.g. **state an opinion, judgement or implication, make a prediction, reiterate viewpoints, make a comment about a change of thinking or belief, pose a question.**

• *How to Revise, Edit and Proofread*

Once students have written the first draft of their investigation, they need to edit their work. Proofreading, editing and revising can be modelled and practised as a whole class before students independently apply these skills to their own work.

Jointly constructing an Editor's Checklist is a good starting point so students can develop these skills.

Being able to answer the following questions may help students process and organise information.

Questions for Students to Consider

- Have I sorted all of my information into headings that will answer the focus questions?
- Do I have all the information I need? If not, what else do I need?
- Where could I go to find this information?
- Have I selected a familiar text form to use?
- Have I combined my sentences logically into paragraphs?
- Is there variety in my sentence leads and length?
- Does my investigation flow, with all the paragraphs logically sequenced and linked?
- Have I included 'my voice' into the piece so that it is not just a regurgitation of factual information?
- Have I edited and revised my text to make sure that the information and ideas are clear?
- Have I proofread my work for spelling, punctuation and grammar?
- Is my bibliography up to date?

Figure 4.57 Questions for Students to Consider

Supporting Students to Process and Organise Information

Teachers can select from the following guided practice activities that will assist students to process and organise information.

1 **Physical Sentence Construction**
2 **Reconstructing a Text**
3 **From None to Some**
4 **Hook, Line and Sinker**
5 **Group Editing**
6 **Editor's Checklist**
7 **Oral Editing**
8 **Main Idea Sort**
9 **Main Idea Pyramid**
10 **Great Debate**

1 Physical Sentence Construction

This activity is designed to help students understand the concept of a sentence and the function of words and punctuation within a sentence.

- Create some cards containing words that can be made into a sentence. Place one word per card, all written in lower case. Put a stick-on note with the initial letter of the word written as a capital on the back of each card.
- Prepare some cards with punctuation marks, one mark per card.
- Have a supply of blank cards and markers ready.
- Hand out out the individual word cards to students.
- Ask those students with cards to form themselves into a sentence at the front of the class.
- Have the whole class read the sentence. Pose the questions "Is this a sentence?" As students offer suggestions such as "It needs to start with a capital letter" have the student holding that card, place their capital letter at the beginning of the word.
- If suggestions are made for punctuation, distribute the suggested punctuation card to a student and have them join the sentence.
- Re-read and check the sentence at each stage.
- Have students suggest how the sentence could be re-arranged or added to. Try some of the suggestions using blank cards to write new or alternative words on to be added to the sentence. Sometimes students need assistance to reduce sentences rather than expand them so this activity can be adapted by having students suggest words to be deleted without altering the meaning of the sentence.

Figure 4.58 Word Cards for Physical Sentence Construction

2 Reconstructing a Text

Reconstructing a Text requires students to manipulate sections of a text to achieve the best effect. Students require an understanding of the structure and function of texts, sentences and paragraphs.

- Provide groups of students with an envelope that contains a text cut into sections. This could be a sentence cut into individual words, a paragraph cut into individual sentences or a text cut into paragraphs.

- Have students read each section and order the text according to what they believe is the most effective.
- Have students share reconstructions with other groups. They can explain their reasons for structuring their text.
- Invite students to compare their reconstruction with the original text.

3 From None to Some

The activity From None to Some reinforces the importance of paragraphing as an organisational tool, both from a writer and reader's viewpoint.

- Have students work with a partner. Provide each pair with a continuous text that does not contain paragraphs.
- Have students read the text and highlight where they think each new paragraph may begin.
- Have pairs share their work with another pair, comparing and justifying choices made.
- Jointly construct a chart, listing how a paragraph links to the next.

4 Hook, Line and Sinker

The Hook, Line and Sinker activity focuses students' attention on headlines and leads in paragraphs. In this activity, students recognise how to identify devices that are used for effect.

- Collect a variety of newspaper or magazine articles. Separate the headline, by line or lead sentence, from the text.
- Arrange students into pairs or small groups. Distribute two or three headlines, bylines or lead sentences to each group.
- Provide time for students to discuss their headlines, encouraging them to speculate on the content of the information to follow.
- Distribute the text and have students match it to the heading, byline or lead sentence.
- Discuss what makes an effective headline or lead sentence. List suggestions that will assist students when they are creating effective opening sentences, e.g. **posing a question, creating a title with a double meaning.**

5 Group Editing

Group Editing involves students collaboratively reviewing a piece of text and making the necessary changes to enhance it.

- Allocate a first draft to each group of students.
- Have students read the piece and make changes.
- Provide opportunities for the whole class to compare and discuss the changes made.

6 Editor's Checklist

Jointly creating an Editor's Checklist supports students in developing the skills needed to independently edit their own work and that of others.

- During modelled, shared and guided writing, jointly construct an editing checklist that includes common proofreading marks, e.g. spelling error ⓈⓅ, ^ insert a word, # insert space.
- Encourage students to refer to and use the checklist during independent writing time and editing sessions.

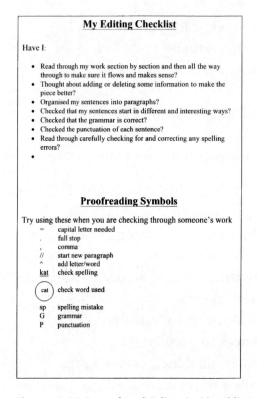

Figure 4.59 Sample of Editor's Checklist

7 Oral Editing

Oral Editing provides an opportunity for students to self-edit as they share their work with a partner. It also provides a chance to receive feedback from an audience.

- Organise students to meet in pairs. Direct students to bring their work to be edited to the meeting.
- Have one student from each pair read their work aloud. Allow the student to stop and make changes as they go. Discuss their work with their partner as needed.
- Encourage students to re-read the corrected sections.
- Once the reading is completed, have the partner offer constructive feedback.
- Repeat the process for the other student in the pair.

The following activities are explained in detail in this book, Chapter 4, Section 1—Teaching Comprehension and Word Identification Strategies.

8 Main Idea Sort
9 Main Idea Pyramid

At this stage in the Information Process, students should have their notes and completed the activity that relates to clustering cards into the pyramid.

10 Great Debate

Step 5—Creating and Sharing a Presentation

The fifth step in the Information Process requires students to create an effective presentation to share their investigation. When creating the presentation, students need to consider the purpose, the information to be shared and the audience. With these factors in mind, it is important that students see that the presentation format for the investigation is not the first decision to be made but one that could evolve as they collect information and gain greater understanding of their investigation.

Many options can be explored for creating and presenting the investigation. Students can be encouraged to explore the print and non-print media options available. Information Technology can be incorporated effectively throughout the entire Information Process and is particularly useful at this stage. Students need to be encouraged to reflect on their own strengths and learning styles as well as considering their audience as they set about selecting a presentation format.

What Students Need to Know

To successfully create and share a presentation, students will need to know about the following:

• *Text Form Knowledge*

Continue to build students' knowledge about the structure, organisation and language features of a range of oral, visual and written text forms. Students can consider using text features that enhance the navigation of an investigation, e.g. **contents, index, glossary, headings, captions, icons**.

• *Use of Information Technology*

A variety of information technology skills will enable students to make choices to enhance their presentations.

Useful computer skills include word processing, charting, creating spreadsheets, and databases and designing web pages. Students can be taught how to use clip art and specialist packages such as Power Point, Hyper Studio and Desk Top Publishing.

Learning how to use specialist audio and visual equipment as well as the creating of sound and images may also be beneficial.

• *Presenting to an Audience*

Decisions about how investigations will be presented will include whether students choose oral, visual or printed modes. Each mode requires different skills.

When presenting in the oral mode, students will benefit from:
– knowing how to use their voices effectively, e.g. **volume, tone, pace, clarity**
– being aware of and responding to the audience e.g. *body language*
– considering the audience involvement
– knowing how to use aids to enhance their presentation
– developing effective introductions and closures
– responding to questions.

When presenting in the visual and written modes, students will benefit from knowing about presentation techniques such as:
– layout and design, e.g. **story boards**
– formats, e.g. **scrolls, charts, models, mobiles, book**
– special effects, e.g. **cut-outs, pop ups**
– borders and lettering.

Being able to answer the following questions may help students create and present an investigation.

Questions for Students to Consider

- What would be the most effective presentation format to use?
- Am I comfortable with the information in my presentation?
- Do I understand all the information in my presentation?
- Do I have a time line and a deadline to create my presentation?
- Do I need to include any text features that will enhance my final presentation, e.g. *illustrations, captions, tables, graphs, maps or diagrams?*
- Do I have the necessary skills to create the presentation I would like to make?
- Do I have a time limit for the presentation of my investigation?
- Have I got someone to give me feedback on my presentation idea including the possible design before I do the final format?
- Is my presentation original?
- Will I need any special resources or equipment for my presentation?
- Have I practised my presentation so that I am familiar with the content and format?

Figure 4.60 Questions for Students to Consider

Supporting Students to Create and Share a Presentation

Teachers can select from the following guided practice activities that will assist students to create and share a presentation

1 **Outlining**
2 **Design This!**

1 Outlining

This activity enables students to investigate text layout and how the placement of text and other features can enhance the readability of a presentation, thereby creating an impact.

• Provide groups of students with pages from a variety of texts.
• Provide time for students to discuss the pages in terms of their visual impact and appeal. Have students justify their comments by pointing out particular features.
• Have each student select one page of text. Use laminated sheeting or overhead projector film to make an outline around the different sections of the text. Direct students to label the text, illustrations and headings.
• Have the students look at the proportion of text to non-text features. Discuss the amount of text versus visual features and their opinions of the effect and appeal of the pages.

2 Design This!

The Design This activity encourages students to create a text layout and design to suit a particular audience.

• Provide groups of students with a jumbled piece of text. (Prior to distributing this text to students, remove any organisational features such as headings or graphics.)
• Allocate an audience and/or context to each group, e.g. **younger students, high school students, adults, text book, women's magazine, newspaper supplement.**
• Have students organise the text into a suitable order. They can then work on the editing and laying out of the text so it will be suitable for their allocated audience.
• Have students add headings, graphics and any other text features that will enhance the appeal and readability for their audience.
• Have students share their text with the whole class, discussing their rationale for design features and text alterations.

Step 6—Evaluating the Investigation

The final step in the Information Process involves students in evaluating the way the investigation was carried out and the effectiveness of their presentation. Evaluation provides an opportunity for students to identify areas of strength and areas for improvement.

For teachers, this is a time to reflect on the overall performance of the student. This includes an evaluation of the processes involved in the investigation as well as the final product. Assessment tools that can be used at this stage include conferences, interviews, surveys and questionnaires.

It is important to note that even though evaluating is listed as the final step in the Information Process, it is, in fact, an ongoing process. Students can be reflecting and evaluating throughout their investigation and their progress can then be monitored.

What Students Need to Know

If students have a clear understanding of the expectations of an investigation from the outset, they can assess their own performance throughout the process.

In order to measure their own performance, students may need to have an understanding of and be able to use a variety of self-assessment tools. These include:
• goal-setting formats
• learning logs
• journals
• reflection sheets
• jointly constructed rubrics and checklists.

Students also benefit from knowing how to provide feedback to their peers.

It is important for students to know how to review the goals they set at the beginning of their investigation. The attainment of these goals can be used to identify strengths and areas of need. They can also be used as the basis for setting future goals.

Being able to answer the following questions may help students evaluate an investigation.

Questions for Students to Consider

- What did I set out to achieve with this investigation?
- Did I achieve all that I wanted to? If no, what stopped me from achieving my goals?
- What new knowledge and skills do I have after completing my investigation?
- Do I think others learnt something through the sharing of my investigation?
- Did I respond to the feedback I received from others?
- If I could do the investigation again, is there anything I would do differently? Why?
- When it comes to the Information Process, what do I think are my strengths?
- What area/s of the Information Process do I need to work on improving?
- As a result of this investigation, what more would I like to know?

Figure 4.61 Questions for Students to Consider

Supporting Students to Evaluate an Investigation

Teachers can select from the following guided practice activities that will assist students to evaluate an investigation.

1 **Two Stars and a Wish**
2 **Journals and Reflection Sheets**
3 **Post a Goal**

1 Two Stars and a Wish

The Two Stars and a Wish activity provides a framework for peers and teachers to give constructive feedback. The activity also promotes active and reflective listening.

This activity can also be used for personal reflection. Comments can be made on positive aspects of work as well as focusing on areas for improvement.

- Before students present their investigation, have them share, with the audience, those aspects on which they would like feedback.
- After the presentation, have the audience respond in the form of two positive comments (stars) and one constructive comment (wish). This can be done in an oral or written form.

2 Journals and Reflection Sheets

Journals and Reflection Sheets can be used by students to reflect on their progress. These journals and sheets promote metacognitive thinking processes.

• At pre-designated points in the Information Process, provide students with a framework that can be used to reflect on their progress. This may be in the form of a series of questions or sentence stems.

3 Post a Goal

The Post a Goal activity helps students to set manageable and achievable goals for themselves and promotes metacognitive thinking.

• Provide students with the Post a Goal framework and have them reflect on various aspects of the Information Process. This may include reviewing aspects that were done well, those aspects that show improvement and those aspects that need improvement.

• Prior to beginning a new investigation, have students return to their reflections so they can use the information to set a plan for improvement.

Parents and the Information Process

It is important that parents be informed about the Information Process and the rationale behind it. It is important for parents to know the teacher's expectations for the investigation as well as being aware that the process is as important as the final product.

Part of informing parents is sharing with them the support role they can play at home. The more informed parents are about the processes and the outcomes to be achieved by students, the more likely parents will understand that their role is one of support and guidance rather than the 'doer' of the investigation.

Parents can be provided with information through letters, parent evenings, newsletters, emails and meetings. Information can be provided to parents about the steps of the Information Process, the teacher's role and the expected role parents can play at home. The key role for parents in supporting their child is one of monitoring their efforts at home and providing feedback to the teacher on any aspects they feel may need extra assistance.

Another aspect to share with parents is the expected amount of time that will be spent on the investigation at school and at home.

Sending home a calendar or a timeline for the investigation with key dates marked for completion of certain tasks is a good way of letting parents and students know the time frame for the investigation. This also inform both parents and students of key completion points along the way. A calendar or timeline will also help students to plan and carry out their investigation in manageable stages, instead of in a rush as the end date approaches.

Inviting parents to observe their child's presentation is another way of including them in the process.

Glossary

alphabetic principle	the assumption underlying alphabetic writing systems that each speech sound or phoneme of the language should have its own distinctive graphic representation
alliteration	the repetition of the initial sound in consecutive words often used to create tongue twisters, e.g. She sells sea shells by the seashore
analysing	a teaching and learning practice involving the examination of the parts to understand the whole
applying	a teaching and learning practice involving the independent use of a skill or strategy to achieve a purpose
assonance	the repetition of vowel sounds often used in lines of poetry, e.g. Ousted from the house, the mongrel growled and howled
cloze procedure	an instructional activity involving the completion of incomplete sentences
compound word	a word as a single unit of meaning but made up of two complete words, e.g. buttonhole, football
concepts of print	understandings about what print represents and how it works, e.g. has a consistent directionality, is made up of letters, words
consonant	one of all the letters of the alphabet except a, e, i, o, u
consonant cluster	a sequence of two or more consonants, e.g. tr, shr, ng
Contextual Understanding	a substrand of reading that involves an understanding of how the context affects the interpretation and choices made by authors and illustrators
continuant sounds	a speech sound produced as an uninterrupted air flow, e.g. /m/, /s/
Conventions	a substrand of reading that focuses on the structures and features of texts, including spelling, grammar, pronunciation and layout
conventions of print	rules that govern the customary use of print in a language, e.g. punctuation, upper and lower case letters
critical literacy	the analysis and questioning of texts to reveal the values and beliefs that attempt to position the users
DEAR	Drop Everything and Read; a name for silent independent reading
deconstructing	analysing a text, section by section, to reveal its structure, linguistic features or use of language
digraph	two letters that together represent one speech sound, e.g. ch, ai, ee, sh
DIRT	Daily Independent Reading Time; a name for silent independent reading
discussing	a teaching and learning practice involving the exchange of opinions on topics, themes or issues
familiarising	a teaching and learning practice involving raising awareness and activating prior knowledge

fish bowl	a modelling technique that involves students seated around the perimeter of the room, observing two or three groups of students rehearsing a process
flexible grouping	groups formed and dissolved depending on the goal of a lesson
fluency	reading aloud smoothly, easily and with expression, showing understanding of the author's message
Global Statement	a written snapshot of a learner in a particular phase of development, which encapsulates the typical characteristics of that phrase
graphic organisers	visual representations of concepts that enable a learner to visualise, record and retrieve information from a text
guiding	a teaching and learning practice involving the provision of scaffolds through strategic assistance at predetermined checkpoints in the learning process
Indicator	a description of a literacy behaviour on the *First Steps* Maps of Development
innovating	a teaching and learning practice involving the alteration or amendment of a text to create a new one
interrogating	questioning and challenging a text to ascertain the underlying values and beliefs
investigating	a teaching and learning practice involving finding, analysing, questioning and using of information for a purpose
Key Indicator	a description of literacy behaviours that most students display at a phase on the *First Steps* Maps of Development
Major Teaching Emphases	teaching priorities appropriate to phases of development
modelling	a teaching and learning practice involving explicit demonstration of the thinking behind how and why something is done
orthographic knowledge	knowing about the spelling of words in a given language according to established usage
orthography	the study of the nature and use of symbols in a writing system, e.g. **letter patterns**
phase	a clustering of behaviours along the *First Steps* Maps of Development
phonogram	see rime, also known as word families, e.g. **at, -ame, -og**
phonology	the study of the sounds in a language;
playing	a teaching and learning practice involving the exploration of concepts and skills through imagining and creating
positioning	an attempt on the part of the author to influence the reader to take a particular point of view
practising	a teaching and learning practice involving the rehearsal of a skill or strategy
Processes and Strategies	a substrand of reading involving the application of knowledge and understandings to comprehend and compose texts

reading conference	a structured conversation in which aspects of students' reading development are discussed
reflecting	a teaching and learning practice involving thinking back on the what, how and why of experiences
rime	a vowel and any following consonants of a syllable, e.g. 'uck' in 'truck'
schwa	an unstressed mid-central vowel as in the first sound in the word 'alone'
sharing	a teaching and learning practice that involves the joint construction of meaning, e.g. between teacher and student, or student and student
simulating	a teaching and learning practice involving the adoption of a role or imagining oneself in a hypothetical setting
situational context	factors such as the purpose of communication, the subject matter of a text; the text form and the roles and relationships between the communication participants that have an impact on the choice of language used in a text
socio–cultural	a combination of social and cultural factors such as economic status, geographical location, beliefs and values
socio–cultural context	the expectations and values of the social and cultural groups at the time a text was written that have an impact on the language used
SSR	Sustained Silent Reading; a name for silent independent reading
stop sounds	a consonant speech sound made by stopping the flow of air, e.g. /b/, /d/, /g/
strand	one of four interwoven language modes, e.g. reading, writing, viewing, speaking and listening
strategy	the mental processes 'you use to do something you want to do'
substrand	one of four interwoven lenses through which student performance in literacy can be monitored and supported, e.g. Use of Texts, Contextual Understanding, Conventions, Processes and Strategies
text	any communication from which meaning is gained, e.g. books, videos, internet web site, conversation
transforming	a teaching and learning practice involving the re-creation of a text in another form, mode or medium, e.g. a story to a play, a book to a film
Use of Texts	a substrand of reading involving the composition and comprehension of texts
USSR	Uninterrupted Sustained Silent Reading; a name for silent independent reading
vowels	a, e, i, o, u, sometimes referred to as long or short; long vowels represent the sound of their letter name, e.g. bay, bee as in boat; short vowels represent the sounds heard in bat, bit, bet, but, bot
word identification	determining the pronunciation and meaning of an unknown word
word recognition	knowing the pronunciation and meaning of words previously encountered

Bibliography

Allen, J. 1999, *Words, Words, Words—Teaching Vocabulary in Grades 4–12*, Stenhouse Publishers, Portland, Maine, USA.

Armbruster, B. B., Lehr, F., and Osborn, J. 2001, *Put Reading First: Research Building Blocks for Teaching Children to Read*, Center for the Improvement of Early Reading Achievement (CIERA), U.S. Department of Education, Washington D.C., USA.

Bailles, J. (ed.) 1980, *The Reading Bug and How to Catch It*, Ashton Scholastic, Sydney, Australia.

Bamford, R. A. and Kristo, J. V. 2000, *Checking Out Nonfiction K–8: Good Choices For Best Learning*, Christopher-Gordon Publishers, Norwood, Massachusetts, USA.

Bartel, B. 1993/1994, 'What research has to say about instruction in text-marking strategies', *Forum for reading*, vol. 24, pp. 11–19.

Bartlett, B. J. 1978, 'Top-level structure as an organisational strategy for recall of classroom text', (unpublished Doctoral Dissertation), Arizona State University, USA.

Beck, I. Dr 2001, 'Word Building Sounds' www.education.pitt.edu/leaders/ Decode%20strategs/wordbuildingsounds.htm Downloaded 27. 08. 2003.

Bishop, W. and Zemliansky, P. 2001, *The Subject Is Research—Processes and Practices*, Boynton/Cook Publishers, Portsmouth, NH, USA.

Bloom, B. S. (ed.) 1956, *Taxonomy of Educational Objectives: The Classification of Educational Goals: Handbook I, Cognitive Domain*, Longmans Green, New York, USA.

Bolton, F. and Snowball, D, 1993, *Teaching Spelling: a Practical Resource*, Thomas Nelson Publishers, South Melbourne, Australia.

Booth D (ed.) 1996, *Literacy Techniques for Building Successful Readers and Writers*, Stenhouse Publishers, York, Maine, USA.

Bransford, J., Brown, A., and Cocking, R., (eds) 1999, *How People Learn: Brain, Mind, Experience and School*. National Research Council, National Academy Press, Washington D.C., USA.

Brian, J. 1991, *Natural Disasters*, Era Publications, Flinders Park, SA, Australia.

Burke, J. 2002, *Tools for Thought—Graphic Organizers for Your Classroom*, Heinemann, Portsmouth, NH, USA.

———— 2000, *Reading Reminders—Tools, Tips and Techniques*, Boynton/Cook Publishers, Portsmouth, NH, USA.

———— 1999, *I Hear America Reading*, Heinemann, Portsmouth, NH, USA.

Byrne, D., Garner. I., Gregory, M., Scott, C and Tierney, G. (compiled by) 1987, *Record Information—Notemaking Methods And Strategies*, Library Services Branch, Education Department Western Australia, Australia.

Cole, A. D. 2003, *Knee to Knee, Eye to Eye—Circling In on Comprehension*, Heinemann, Portsmouth, NH, USA.

Creenaune, T. and Rowles, L. 1996, *What's Your Purpose? Reading Strategies for Non-Fiction Texts*, Primary English Teaching Association, Marrickville, NSW, Australia.

Cunningham, P. M. 2000, *Phonics They Use*, Addison-Wesley Educational Publishers, New York, USA.

———— & Allington, R. 1999, *Classrooms that Work*, Addison-Wesley Educational Publishers, New York, USA.

Daniels, H. 1994, *Literature Circles Voice and Choice in the Student-Centered Classroom*, Stenhouse, Maine, USA.

Dansereau, D. F. (1980) 'Learning strategy research', Paper presented at NEI-LRDC Conference on Thinking and Learning Skills, Pittsburg, PA, USA.

Day, C. (2003) 'Reading and responding in literature circles', *PEN 140*, PETA, NSW, Australia.

Dee-Lucas, D., and Larkin, J. H. 1990, 'Organisation and comprehensibility in scientific proofs or consider a article p...' *Journal of Educational Psychology*, 82 (4), 701–714.

Department for Education and Employment, 1998, *The National Literacy Strategy—Framework for Teaching*, DfEE, Sudbury, Suffolk, UK.

Dolch, E W. 1939, *A Manual for Remedial Reading*, Garrard Press, Champaign, Illinois, USA.

Duffelmeyer, F., Baum, D.D. and Merkley, D.J. 1987, 'Maximizing reader-text confrontation with an extended anticipation guide', *Journal of Reading*, 31, pp. 146–150.

Edelen-Smith, P, 1997, 'How now brown cow: phonic awareness activities for collaborative classrooms', *Intervention in School and Clinic*, vol. 33, Number 2.

Education Department of Western Australia 2001, *Success for All—Selecting Appropriate Learning Strategies*, Curriculum Corporation, Carlton South, Vic, Australia.

_____ 1983, *First Sounds*, Government Print, Perth, Western Australia.

_____ 1999 *Shared and Guided Reading and Writing 2*, GHPD, Oxford UK.

Ehri, L. C. 1998, 'Research on learning to read and spell: a personal historical perspective', *Scientific Studies of Reading* vol. 2, pp. 97–114.

Erickson, J. and Lehrer, R (in press), 'The Evolution of Critical Standards As Students Design Hypermedia Design', *Journal of the Learning Sciences* (special issue on learning through problem solving) vol. 7. Nos 3 & 4.

Fielding, L., Pearson, D., 1994, 'Reading Comprehension: What Works', *Educational Leadership*, pp. 62–68.

Firmstone, G., Tuffield, G., Toon, F., and Firmstone, N., 1996, *Strategic Spelling*, Rigby Heinemann, Melbourne, Australia.

Fox, B. and Routh, D. K 1975, 'Analysing spoken language into words, syllables and phonemes: A developmental study', *Journal of Psycholinguistic Research*, vol. 4, pp. 331–342.

French, R. and Whitaker, J. 1996, *Realising Literacy Through Projects*, Primary English Teaching Association, Newtown, NSW, Australia.

Fry, E., Kness, J. and Fountoukidis, D. 1984, *The Reading Teacher's Book of Lists*, Prentice Hall, Paramus, New Jersey, USA.

Goodman, K. 1996, *Ken Goodman On Reading—A Common-sense Look at the Nature of Language and the Science of Reading*, Heinemann, Portsmouth, NH, USA.

Goswami, U. 1994, 'Reading by analogy: theoretical and practical perspectives', C. Hulme and M. Snowling (eds), *Reading Development and Dyslexia*, Whurr, London, pp.18–30.

Granada Learning, 1999, *Talking About Information & Communications Technology in Subject Teaching—A Guide for Teachers Secondary KS3 & KS4*, Canterbury Christ Church University College, Canterbury, Kent, UK.

Graves, M., and Graves, B. 1994, *Scaffolding Reading Experiences: Designs for Student Success*, Christopher Gordon, Norwood, MA, USA.

Gray, L. 1995, *My Mamma Had a Dancing Heart*, Orchard Books, New York, USA.

Green, P. 1992, *A Matter of Fact—Using Factual Texts in the Classroom*, Eleanor Curtin Publishing, Armadale, Vic, Australia.

Griffiths, A. 2002, *The Day My Bum Went Psycho*, Pan Macmillan, Australia.

Harney, S. 1992, *A Dinosaur Directory*, Jacaranda Press, Queensland, Australia.

Harris, T. L. and Hodges, R. E. (eds.) 1995, *The Literacy Dictionary*, International Reading Association, Newark, Delaware, USA.

Harvey, S. 1998, *Nonfiction Matters—Reading, Writing and Research in Grades 3–8*, Stenhouse Publishers, York, Maine, USA.

_____ & Goudvis A. 2000, *Strategies That Work—Teaching Comprehension to Enhance Understanding*, Stenhouse Publishers, York, Maine, USA.

Herber, H. L 1970, *Teaching Reading in Content Areas*, Prentice-Hall, Englewood Cliffs, NJ, USA.

Hooper, M. 1995, *Looking After the Egg*, Ginn and Company, Aylesbury, Bucks, UK.

Hoyt, L., Moonye, M. and Parkes, B. (eds.) 2003, *Exploring Informational Texts—From Theory to Practice*, Heinemann, Portsmouth, NH, USA.

_____ 2002, *Make It Real—Strategies for Success with Informational Texts*, Heinemann, Portsmouth, NH, USA.

_____ 1999, *Revisit, Reflect, Retell—Strategies for Improving Reading Comprehension*, Heinemann, Portsmouth, NH, USA.

_____ 2000, *Snapshots—Literacy Minilessons Up Close*, Heinemann, Portsmouth, NH, USA.

http://www.education-world.com/a_lesson/lesson035.shtml Downloaded 15/09/03

International Reading Association 1998, *Phonemic Awareness and the Teaching of Reading—A Position Statement from the Board of Directors of the International Reading Association*, International Reading Association, Newark, Delaware, USA.

Johnson, D. 1999, *Designing Research Projects Students (and Teachers) Love*, Information Today Inc. http://www.infotoday.com/MMSchools/nov99/johnson.htm Downloaded 10/06/02.

_____ & Pearson P. D., 1984, *Teaching Reading Vocabulary*, CBS College Publishing, NY, USA.

Jose, E. and Andersen, H. C. 1989, *Little Match Girl: A Classic Tale*, Phyliis Fogelman Books, New York, USA.

Juel, C. Griffith, P. and Gough, P. 1986, 'Acquisition of literacy: A longitudinal study of children in first and second grade', *Journal of Educational Psychology*, vol. 78, pp. 243–255.

Kajder, S. B. 2003, *The Tech-Savvy English Classroom*, Stenhouse Publishers, Portland, Maine, USA.

Keene, E.O., Zimmerman. S. 1997, *Mosaic of Thought—Teaching Comprehension in a Reader's Workshop*, Heinemann, Portsmouth, New Hampshire. USA.

Leonhardt, M., 1993, *Parents Who Love Reading, Kids Who Don't*, Crown Trade Paperbacks, New York, USA.

Lyon, A. and Moore, P. 2003, *Sound Systems*, Stenhouse, Portland, Maine, USA.

Lyon, G. R. 1997, 'Statement of G. Reid Lyon to the Committee on Education and the Workforce', 19 July 1997, National Institute of Child Health and Human Development, U.S. House of Representatives Washington D.C.

McAlexander, P., & Burrell, K. 1996, 'Helping Students "Get It Together" with synthesis journals', (Paper presented at the annual conference of the National Association of Developmental Education, Little Rock, AR.).

McKenzie, J. 2000, *Beyond Technology—Questioning, Research and the Information Literate School*, FNO Press, Bellingham, Washington D.C., USA.

McKeown, M. G. and Beck I. L. 1988, 'Learning Vocabulary: Different Ways for Different Goals, Remedial and Special Education' (*RASE*), vol. 9 (issue 1), pp. 42–46.

McLaughlin, M. 2003, *Guided Comprehension in the Primary Grades*, International Reading Association, Newark, Delaware, USA.

_____ & Allen, M. B. 2002, *Guided Comprehension—A Teaching Model for Grades 3–8*, International Reading Association, Newark, Delaware, USA.

_____ 2002, *Guided Comprehension in Action—Lessons for Grades 3–8*, International Reading Association, Newark, Delaware, USA.

McMackin, D. C. and Siegel, B .S. 2002, *Knowing How—Researching and Writing Nonfiction 3–8*, Stenhouse Publishers, York, Maine, USA.

Marshall, N., and Glock, M. 1979, 'Comprehension of connected discourse: A study into the relationships between structure of a text and information recalled', *Reading Research Quarterly*, Vol. 16, pp. 10–56.

Methold, K. 1981, *In a Nutshell—A Guide to Mastering Summary Skills*, Longman Cheshire, Melbourne, Vic, Australia.

Meyer, B. J. F., 1975, *Identification of the Structure of Prose and Its Implications for the Study of Reading and Memory*, Journal of Reading Behaviour, Vol 7, No 1, 7–47.

Meyer, B. J. F. 1985, 'Prose analysis: Purposes, procedures and problems', from *Understanding Expository Text* B. Britton & J. Black. (eds.), Hillsdale, NJ: Erlbaum, (pp. 11–64).

Meyer B.J.F., Brandt, D.M., and Bluth, G.J., 1978, 'Use of Author's Schema: Key to Ninth Grade's Comprehension', paper presented at meeting of the American Educational Research Association, Toronto, Canada.

_____ and Freedle, R., 1979, *The Effects of Different Discourse Topic on Recall*, Educational Testing Service, Princeton, New Jersey, USA

Miller, D. 2002, *Reading with Meaning—Teaching Comprehension in the Primary Grades*, Stenhouse Publishers, Portland, Maine, USA.

Morris, A. and Stewart-Dore, N. 1984, *Learning to Learn from Text Effective Reading in the Content Area*, Addison-Wesley, Australia.

Moustafa, M. 1997, *Beyond Traditional Phonics—Research Discoveries and Reading Instruction*, Heinemann, Portsmouth, NH, USA.

Nagy, W. E., et al. 1985, *Learning Word Meanings from Context: How Broadly Generalizable?* Technical Report No. 347. Urbana, IL, Center for the Study of Reading.

Neate, B. 1992, *Finding out about Finding Out—A Practical Guide to Children's Information Books*, Infopress, Winchester, UK.

Neely, M. 1996, *The Australian Internet Guide for Teachers, Students & Parents* (Second Edition) MaxiBooks, Kiama, NSW, Australia.

Bibliography

Ogle, D. 1986, 'KWL: A teaching model that develops active reading of expository texts', *The Reading Teacher*, International Reading Association, Newark, Delaware, USA, February.

Ohanian, S. 2002, *The Great Word Catalogue—FUNdamental Activities for Building Vocabulary*, Heinemann, Portsmouth, NH, USA.

O'Hear, M.F. 1991, 'Involving students: interactive computing in a reading/study skills course', *Research and Teaching in Developmental Education*, vol. 8 issue 1, pp. 15–20.

Optiz, M. 1998, *Goodbye Round Robin Reading—25 Effective Oral Reading Strategies*, Heinemann, Portsmouth, NH, USA.

_____ 2000, *Rhymes and Reasons—Literature and Language Play for Phonological Awareness*, Heinemann, Portsmouth, NH, USA.

_____ & Ford, M. 2001, *Reaching Readers—Flexible and Innovative Strategies for Guided Reading*, Heinemann, Portsmouth, NH, USA.

Otto, W. and Chester, R. 'Sight words for beginning readers', *Journal of Education Research*, 1972, 65, 435–43.

Palincsar. A. 1984, *The Quest for Meaning from Expository Text—A Teacher Guided Journey*, Longman, New York, USA.

Patterson, K. 1977, *Bridge to Terabithia*, HarperCollins Juvenile Books, New York, USA.

Pearson, P. D. 1976, 'A Psycholinguistic Model of Reading', *Language Arts*, vol. 53. pp. 309–314.

_____ and Gallagher, M. C. 1983, 'The instruction of reading comprehension, *Contemporary Educational Psychology*, vol. 8, pp. 317–344.

Pennac, D. 1992, *Better than Life*, Pembroke Publishers Ltd, Ontario, Canada

Pinnell, G. and Fountas, I. 1998, *Word Matters—Teaching Phonics and Spelling in the Reading/Writing Classroom*, Heinemann, Portsmouth, NH, USA.

_____ 1996, *Guided Reading*, Heinemann, Portsmouth, NH, USA.

_____ & Scharer, P. L. 2003, *Teaching for Comprehension in Reading Grades K–2*, Scholastic Professional Books, New York, NY, USA.

Powell D and Hornsby, D. 1993, *Learning Phonics and Spelling in a Whole Language Classroom*, Scholastic Professional Books, New York, NY, USA.

Raphael, Taffy. E., 1982, 'Question-answer strategies for children', *The Reading Teacher*, International Reading Association, Newark, Delaware, USA, November.

Riley, P. 1995, *Vehicles—The Inside Story*, Ginn and Company, Aylesbury, Bucks, UK.

Robb, L. 1995, *Reading Strategies That Work—Teaching Your Students To Become Better Readers*, Scholastic Professional Books, New York, NY, USA.

Routman, R. 1991, *Invitations*, Heinemann, Portsmouth, NH, USA.

Routman, R. 2000, *Conversations: Strategies for Teaching, Learning, and Evaluating*, Heinemann, Portsmouth, NH, USA.

Rowe, G. and Gray, R. 1992, *It's Easy—Ten steps to writing successful school projects*, Dellasta Pty Ltd, Mt Waverley, Vic, Australia.

Rubinstein, G. (compiled by) 1988, *After Dark—Seven Tales to Read at Night*, Omnibus Books, Norwood, S.A. Australia.

Sadler, C.R. 2001, *Comprehension Strategies for Middle Grade Learners*, International Reading Association, Newark, USA.

Share, D.L. and Stanovich, K.E 1995, 'Cognitive processes in early reading: accommodating individual difference into a mode of acquisition', Issues in Education: Contributions from Educational Psychology, Vol. 1.

Sloan. P., and Latham. R. 1981, *Teaching Reading Is...*, Nelson, Melbourne, Victoria, Australia.

Smith,S.B., Simmons, D.C., and Kame'enui, E. J. 1995, 'Synthesis of Research on phonological awareness: Principles and implications for reading acquisition', *Technical Report No 21*, National Center to Improve the Tools of Education. Eugene: University of Oregon.

Stahl, S.A. and Murray, B.A. (1994) 'Defining phonological awareness and its relationship to early reading', *Journal of Educational Psychology*, vol. 86, pp. 221–234.

Stanovich, K. E. 1986, 'Matthew effects in reading: some consequences of individual differences in the acquisition of literacy', *Reading Research Quarterly*, vol. 21, issue 4.

Stanovich, K.E, Cunningham, A.E and Cramer, B. 1984, 'Assessing Phonological Awareness in Kindergarten Children: issues of task comparability', *Journal of Experimental Child Psychology* vol. 38, pp. 175–190

Stauffer, R., 1980, *The Language Experience Approach to the Teaching of Reading*, 2nd ed, New York, Harper and Row.

The *Sunday Times* 2003, *Fishing WA: Part One: Southern WA*, Perth, Western Australia, Australia.

Thorndyke, P. W. 1977, 'Cognitive structures in comprehension and memory of a narrative discourse', *Cognitive Psychology*, vol 9, pp. 77–110.

Tompkins, G. E. 2001, *Literacy for the 21st century: A Balanced Approach* (Second Edition). Prentice Hall, Upper Saddle River, NJ, USA.

Tompkins, G.E. 1998, *50 Literacy Strategies Step by Step*, Merrill, New Jersey, USA.

Treiman, R. 1993, *Beginning to Spell. A Study of First Grade Children*, Oxford University Press, NY, USA.

Treiman, R. (1992) 'The Role of Intrasyllabic Units in Learning to Read and Spell', in *Reading Acquisition*, eds P. Gough, L.C. Ehri and R. Treiman, Hillsdale, NJ: Lawrence Erlbaum Associates.

Tucker, E., *Spelling Essentials*, R.I.C. Publications, Perth, Western Australia, Australia.

Turner, A. (ed.) 1992, *Patterns of Thinking—Top Level Structure in the Classroom*, Primary English Teaching Association, Newtown, NSW, Australia

Vacca, R. T. & Vacca J. L., 1989, *Content Area Reading 3rd edn*, HarperCollins, New York, USA.

Victorian Department of Education, *Wrapping Up Research Project*, [online] Available http://www.highlands.vic.edu.au/research.html

Ward, G. 1988, *I've Got A Project On...* Primary English Teaching Association, Rozelle, NSW, Australia.

Watson, A. and Badenhop, A. (ed.) 1992 *Prevention of Reading Failure*, Scholastic, NSW, Australia.

Weaver, C., 1994, *Reading Process and Practice*, Heinemann, Portsmouth, NH, USA.

Weckert, C., 1994, *Teaching Reluctant Readers in the Mainstream Classroom*, Scholastic, NSW, Australia

Wilhelm, J.D., Friedemann, P.D. and Erickson J. 1998, *Hyperlearning—Where Projects, Inquiry and Technology Meet*, Stenhouse Publishers, York, Maine, USA.

_____ & Baker. T.N. and Dube J. 2001, *Strategic Reading—Guiding Students to Lifelong Literacy 6–12*, Boynton/Cook Publishers, Portsmouth, NH, USA.

_____ 2001, *Improving Comprehension with Think-Aloud Strategies*, Scholastic Professional Books, New York, NY, USA.

Wilson, L. 2002, *Reading To Live: How to Teach Reading for Today's World*, Heinemann, Portsmouth, NH, USA.

Winch, G., Ross Johnston, R., Holliday, M., Ljungdahl, L. and March, P. (2001) *Literacy: Reading, Writing, and Children's Literature*, Oxford University Press, Port Melbourne, Victoria, Australia.

Worthy, J. & Broaddus, K. 2001, 'Fluency beyond the primary grades: From group performance to silent, independent reading', *The Reading Teacher*, vol. 55, pp. 334–343.

Wylie, R. E and Durrell, D. D 1970 'Teaching vowels through phonograms', *Elementary English*, vol. 47 pp. 787–791.

Zorfass, J. M. and Copel, H. 1998, *Teaching Middle School Students to Be Active Researchers*, Association for Supervision and Curriculum Development, Alexandria, VA, USA.

Zygouris-Coe, V 2001, *FLaRE Document—Phonemic Awareness*, Family and Reading Excellence Center, University of Florida, FL, USA.

First Steps Second Edition Professional Development Courses

The ***First Steps Second Edition*** materials form a critical part of the *First Steps* professional development courses that promote a long-term commitment to educational change. Together, the professional development and the materials provide a strategic whole-school approach to improving students' literacy outcomes.

First Steps offers a full range of professional development courses that are conducted at the invitation of a school or education sector. Given the breadth of literacy, schools generally choose to implement only one strand of literacy at a time. A strand should be selected on a needs basis in line with a school's priorities. Schools can select from two-day courses in any of these strands:
• Reading
• Writing and Spelling
• Viewing
• Speaking and Listening.

Each participant who attends a two-day course receives:
• a Map of Development in the chosen literacy strand
• a Resource Book
• the *Linking Assessment, Teaching and Learning* Book
• a course book of professional development reflections
• practical activities for classroom use.

Within each strand, a selection of additional sessions, beyond the regular course, will also be available to meet the needs of teachers in different schools and contexts. These additional sessions can be selected in consultation with a *First Steps* Consultant.

For further information about or registration in *First Steps* courses contact your nearest STEPS Professional Development Office.

UNITED STATES OF AMERICA
STEPS Professional Development
and Consulting
97 Boston Street
Salem
Massachusetts USA 01970
Phone: 978 744 3001
Fax: 978 744 7003
Toll free: 1866 505 3001
www.stepspd.org

AUSTRALASIA
STEPS Professional Development
65 Walters Drive
Osborne Park WA 6017
Phone: 08 9273 8833
Fax: 08 9273 8811
www.ecurl.com.au

UNITED KINGDOM
STEPS Professional Development
and Consulting
Shrivenham Hundred
Business Park
Majors Road
Watchfield SN8TZ
Phone: 01793 787930
Fax: 01793 787931
www.steps-pd.co.uk

CANADA
STEPS Professional Development
and Consulting
26 Prince Andrew Place
Don Mills Ontario M3C 2T8
Phone: 416 442 3224
Fax: 416 443 0948
Toll free: 1800 667 6942
www.pearsoned.ca